12.60

W9-AFA-018

VGM Careers for You Series

CAREERS FOR

ROMANTICS
& Other
Dreamy Types

Blythe Camenson

VGM Career Horizons
NTC/Contemporary Publishing Group

Library of Congress Cataloging-in-Publication Data

Camenson, Blythe.
    Careers for romantics & other dreamy types / Blythe Camenson.
        p.   cm. — (VGM careers for you series)
        ISBN 0-8442-2962-8 (cloth). — ISBN 0-8442-2963-6 (pbk.)
        1. Vocational guidance—United States. 2.   I. Title.
    II. Series.
    HF5382.5.U5C2519   1999
    331.7′02′0973—dc21   99–28740
                                                               CIP

To Charlie Bradley,
for showing me what
romance really means

Published by VGM Career Horizons
A division of NTC/Contemporary Publishing Group, Inc.
4255 West Touhy Avenue, Lincolnwood (Chicago), Illinois 60712-1975 U.S.A.
Copyright © 2000 by NTC/Contemporary Publishing Group, Inc.
Printed in the United States of America
International Standard Book Number: 0-8442-2962-8 (cloth)
                                                  0-8442-2963-6 (paper)
    01   02   03   04   05   LB   18   17   16   15   14   13   12   11   10   9   8   7   6   5   4   3   2   1

Contents

TM

Acknowledgments

The author would like to thank the following romantics for providing information about their careers:

Barry Brand, Flower Grower, Carpinteria, California

Garry Hickerson, Great Expectations, Schaumburg, Illinois

Robyn Carr, Writer, Higley, Arizona

Tom Doyle, Palmetto Carriage Works, Charleston, South Carolina

Charlene Dunn, American Floral Services, Oklahoma City, Oklahoma

Sherry Ebertshauser, Caterer, Louisville, Kentucky

Mary Fallon Miller, Travel Agent, St. Petersburg, Florida

Frances Haberkost, Caterer, Akron, Ohio

Mary Kern, Makeup Artist, Wall, New Jersey

Donna Lemire, Illusions Bridal Shop, Tyngsboro, Massachusetts

Kathleen Lucerne, Cosmetologist, Sunrise, Florida

Al Mendoza, Florist, Floral Designer, Dolton, Illinois

Michael O'Donnell, O'Donnell Farms, Coconut Creek, Florida

Richard Pearlman, Richard Pearlman Chocolates, Berkeley, California

Vivian Portela Buscher, Travel Agent, Miami, Florida

Pat Reese, Flower Broker, Hampshire, Illinois

Ronald Rice, Ron Rice Photography, Torrance, California

Roger and Mary Schmidt, Innkeepers, Nantucket, Massachusetts

Colleen Taber, Flower Importer, Pembroke Pines, Florida

Mary Tribble, Mary Tribble Creations, Charlotte, North Carolina

Tad Wojnicki, Writer, Carmel, California

CHAPTER ONE

Gaze Over the Options

D o you look at the world through rose-colored glasses? Do you love being in love—or being around other people who are? Do old movies make you cry? Would nothing please you more than a moonlit night, a romantic carriage ride, a jug of wine, and thou?

If you answered yes to any of those questions, you are a true romantic. And what could be better than finding a job that allows you to combine your romantic instincts with a way to make a living?

In *Careers for Romantics*, you will find a selection of professions with a variety of background and training requirements, but they all have one common thread—they're ideal for the dreamy romantic.

Career Possibilities for Romantics

Romantics possess qualities above and beyond their dreamy natures, and they are as diverse as the areas of interests to explore. Some are thrilled to find an outlet for their creative talents; others enjoy working with their hands or manipulating words. Still others find their niches using their organizational and business skills. Certainly, almost all romantics have excellent people skills—a definite plus for most careers.

In this book, we will examine carefully more than a dozen careers that are ideal for romantics. (If you put your thinking cap on, you can probably come up with scores of other options to add to the list.) Some allow you to be independently self-employed; others will suggest possible employers for whom you can work.

Matchmakers

"Matchmaker, matchmaker, make me a match . . ." For some romantics helping others to find their soul mates is a rewarding experience. Perhaps you've already brought together single friends and watched as the romance grew and prospered. Wouldn't it be fun to put this particular talent to good use and make money doing it? All over the country, dating and introduction services have sprung up, providing boundless career opportunities for the talented matchmaker. Chapter 2 will show you all the ins and outs.

Romance Writers

Romance books have captured the largest audience of America's reading public. If you have a way with words and a persistent nature, then Chapter 3 will show you how to get started.

But writing romance novels is not the only outlet for the true romantic. You'll also learn how to start your own creative business, writing love letters for hire.

Flower Power

The floral industry coined the expression "Say it with flowers" years ago, and romantics have been doing just that ever since. For an inside look at the different careers open to flower lovers, turn to Chapter 4.

Chocolate Lovers

Some people think that a good piece of chocolate is better than . . . well, better than most anything else. And, no, this isn't a suggestion to get a job with the Hershey's factory—although, that's not a bad idea at all. In Chapter 5 you'll meet a chocolatier who puts his romantic talents to work, creating unusual gifts designed to bypass the stomach and go right to the heart.

Bridal Finery

Nothing is as beautiful as a glowing bride. Whether designing and selling bridal gowns or veils or helping select gowns for attendants, romantics can find satisfying careers helping brides shine on the special day. See Chapter 6 for a firsthand account from a bridal shop owner.

The Big Event

Nothing is more romantic than a storybook wedding, and though many brides-to-be do all the planning themselves, more and more rely on the services of professionals. In Chapter 6, you'll also see how wedding consultants and event planners make sure the wedding goes off without a hitch.

A Meal To Remember

A romantic meal for two (with a glittering diamond waiting at the bottom of a wine glass) or a catered affair for a wedding party of a hundred or more provide ample opportunities for satisfying careers. Chapter 7 will tell you what a catering career is like.

Beauty Secrets

Before stepping out in front of the camera, the last thing a bride takes care of is her hair and makeup. Opportunities abound for skilled hairstylists and makeup artists to help create a romantic look for a beautiful bride. Read Chapter 8 for inside information on what these careers are like.

Lasting Memories

Photographers and videographers specialize in wedding photography and create lasting memories of these romantic occasions. In Chapter 9, you will learn how to get started in these careers.

The Honeymooners

For every successful honeymoon there is a smiling travel agent behind the scenes, planning and scheduling and ensuring that the newlyweds have a memorable vacation. Out of all the industries worldwide, travel and tourism continue to grow at an astounding rate. Almost everyone hopes to go away for at least one week a year, and anniversary and post-wedding trips make up the bulk of those trips. This provides ideal career possibilities for romantics with an interest in travel and a flair for detail. See Chapter 10 to learn how to get started in the travel business.

Idyllic Hideaways

Most people see operating a bed-and-breakfast or historic inn as a romantic enterprise, but successful romantics also have to have a practical side to their natures. Although patrons might view the hideaway experience as romantic—and it certainly is—it is also a business that requires hard work and long hours, as well as healthy start-up capital. If retiring to an out-of-the-way place and running your own inn has always been your dream, read in Chapter 10 how another couple made a go of it.

Romantic Rides

What romantic honeymoon would be complete without an old-fashioned carriage ride through the park on a moonlit night? In Chapter 10, you'll meet an entrepreneur who put his romantic instincts to work in a successful horse and buggy concession.

Choosing Your Field

People involved with romantic work give of themselves in many different capacities, providing a variety of valuable services. If you're reading this book, chances are you're already considering a career in one of the many areas of this fun and wide-open category.

But perhaps you're not sure of the working conditions the different fields offer or which area would suit your personality, skills, and lifestyle the most. There are several factors to consider when deciding which sector to pursue. Each field carries with it different levels of responsibility and commitment. Some also require financial resources to get started. To identify occupations that will match your expectations, you need to know what each job entails.

Ask yourself the following questions and make note of your answers. Then, as you go through the chapters, compare your requirements to the information provided inside. It will help you pinpoint the fields that would interest you and eliminate those that would clearly be the wrong choice.

• How much time are you willing to commit to training? Some skills can be learned on the job or in a year or two of formal training; others can take considerably longer.

• Do you want to work behind a desk, either at home or in a busy office, or would you prefer to be out and about?

• Can you handle a certain amount of stress on the job, or would you prefer a quiet, work-alone environment?

• How much money do you expect to earn starting out and after you have a few years' experience under your belt? Salaries and earnings vary greatly in each chosen profession.

• How much independence do you require? Do you want to be your own boss or will you be content as a salaried employee?

• Can you pay attention to detail, handle paperwork, bookkeeping, and busy schedules?

Knowing what your expectations are, then comparing them to the realities of the work will help you make informed choices.

The Training You'll Need

The training required for the careers covered in this book vary greatly. Some positions require no more than a high school education. Others demand that you have special talents or creative skills plus some prior work experience.

In the following chapters you will find the requirements for each field.

Earnings

As with training requirements, salaries vary widely from position to position. Factors such as the size of the company or the region of the country can determine salary levels more than job complexity or the level of the candidate's education and experience.

Many of the careers in this book are for those willing to be self-employed. That means having start-up capital available and business know-how to make a good living. How inventive you are and how willing you are to create your own opportunities can affect the size of your income.

For More Information

In Appendix A you will find professional associations for many of the career paths explored in this book. Most offer booklets and pamphlets with career information. Some are free; others might have a nominal charge of one or two dollars. A phone call or letter will have information in the mail to you within a few days.

In addition to professional associations, many reference books exist that are related to the careers discussed in this book. Before embarking upon a new career, it's a good idea to read up on it as much as possible. Turn to Appendix B for more information.

CHAPTER TWO

Matchmakers

D o you ever find yourself saying, "I know just the right guy (or gal) for you?" Perhaps you delight in inviting two (unsuspecting) single friends home to dinner—to meet one another. You love describing the assets of one acquaintance to another, handing out phone numbers, fixing people up, arranging dates. Even more so, you are ecstatic when you hear about one of your chosen couples "clicking"—and you've attended more weddings than you can count. (On the other hand, you can take the heat—you don't cringe and run the other way if the match is a flop.)

Perhaps people refer to you as the "matchmaker" and respect your intuitive powers in bringing just the right people together. Wouldn't it be wonderful if you could combine your natural talents in a career that could bring you a nice income and the satisfaction of a job well done—on a regular basis? No, you'd never think of charging friends for your services—but what about working with people you don't know yet?

It's well known that as we leave school and go out into the world of work, the more difficult it becomes to meet potential mates. There are more than fifty-five million single Americans—and that number is rising all of the time. With so many people following busy careers and often relocating to new cities, no longer can "searching singles" rely on the family matchmaker to provide introductions to suitable mates.

But whenever there is a need, industrious people find a way to fill it. In the last few decades, dating services have sprung up all over the country. You find their announcements on community bulletin boards, in your mailbox, and even on-line.

Fewer than 2 percent of those fifty-five million singles out there belong to a dating service. With a customer base that large, it is not unreasonable to assume that this industry will continue to grow and attract new employees. There probably is a job as a professional matchmaker waiting out there for you right now.

The Different Kinds of Dating Services

The dating services discussed below fall into both the traditional and unusual realms. You can seek these services out (just look in the phone book) for employment opportunities, or you can let them spark a few ideas for starting your own service. If there seems to be too much competition in your location, but you really would love to be your own boss—try narrowing the groups of people for which you would provide introductions. For example, in addition to all the general singles introduction services, think about these possibilities:

- Senior singles

- Alternative-lifestyle singles

- Teen dates

- College students

- Ethnic services (catering to, for example, Jewish, African-American, or Italian-American singles)

- Second-time-around singles (for divorced or widowed individuals)

- Skiing singles (or any other kind of activity or hobby that would bring people with common interests together)

- Legal-eagle singles (or any other kind of profession that would bring people in similar careers together)

Look to the following descriptions to see the various types of services that would let you put your matchmaking talents to good use.

Lunch Dates

As an experienced amateur matchmaker, you probably already know how nervous someone can get when meeting a potential mate for the first time. The day of the week and the time and place of the meeting can, in some respects, add to the nervousness. A Saturday night date often unconsciously creates more pressure than a daytime meeting for lunch. One such service in Boston, Massachusetts, called, simply, LunchDates™, realized that and found a way to put people together in a nonthreatening situation. LunchDates' matchmakers pair up couples by common interests and the other usual criteria—but they add to that the proximity in which the two work to one another. Restaurants are informed of the pending lunch date and are ready to introduce the couple and seat them at a quiet table. With a lunch date, there's no wondering how to quickly bail out if the meeting isn't all the client had hoped for—both people have only an hour for their first get-together, then it's out the door and back to work.

As a counselor for a lunchtime dating service, you would make all the arrangements for clients to meet in a public restaurant without revealing their last names or telephone numbers. After the date, it is up to the clients whether to exchange that information.

With this type of service you can charge clients a fee for a time period of membership or for a limited number of introductions. And you might even earn a percentage of the tab from the restaurants to which you regularly send your customers.

Video Dating Services

"Blind" dates became almost a thing of the past with the introduction of video dating services. Video dating centers bring couples together by allowing them to either videotape a few minutes of themselves or to view videotapes made by other members—or both. These taped accounts give clients a chance to see their prospective mates and hear them talk about themselves—what they are looking for, what is important to them, how they feel about relationships in general, what their interests are. Many people prefer this method of introduction, feeling it adds more depth than a pen-and-paper profile or a two-dimensional photograph.

A typical video dating service center contains a library consisting of an information/service area or front desk, books containing male and female profiles and photos, videos, and a viewing area. There are also interview offices for potential members, a photography and videography studio, and often a separate telemarketing area.

Clients usually pay a membership fee for unlimited access to video libraries. Once a potential date or mate has been identified, the service helps clients contact each other. Here employees usually earn a commission based on a percentage of the membership fee.

Computer Databases

Computer dating services have been around for thirty years or so. Early services provided clients with application forms to fill out with spaces to check off preferences. The client would then mail in the form with the service fee and wait to receive a printout of compatible partners. No photographs were provided, but names and addresses often were, making this method not always the safest route to go.

These days clients can access on-line computer databases, read profiles, place their own profiles, check out the photographs, and respond to a "blind" E-mail address.

Many of these on-line services are free to clients; others charge a small handling fee. Anyone with a computer, a modem, and the know-how to build a website can start an on-line dating service. The know-how isn't even crucial—many different services offer website building and maintenance for a fee. The revenue you earn would come from advertisers and/or sponsors. The more "hits" your site had, the higher you could charge for advertising space.

Telephone Personal Ads

Newspapers routinely run personal ads in their classified sections; some of these newspapers have set up 900 numbers for respondents to reply to ads of interest. Instead of writing to a blind box number, you can listen to each person's voice and leave a message of your own.

Applying to a newspaper personal ad department would be one way to work with this matchmaking endeavor. Another way would be to call the telephone company, arrange for your own 900 number, then start advertising your matchmaking service in appropriate publications. Typically, earnings come from the amount of time the caller spends on the phone—it's up to you to decide how much per minute you would charge.

Different Job Titles
Within Dating Services

Job titles vary from service to service. The size of the service will determine the number of employees and the different roles they will play. In a large enterprise, an employee might specialize in only one aspect of the business; in a small company, one person might perform several functions.

As a general rule of thumb, you will find all or some of the following job descriptions in most dating services.

Directors

No matter what the business, the role of the director is usually the same—to supervise the day-to-day operations of the company, including business practices and staff performance and training. Some directors are also responsible for budgeting, payroll, banking, and other related duties.

Sales Managers

For many dating services, sales is the key. Sales managers direct the firm's sales program. They assign sales territories and goals and establish training programs for their sales representatives. Managers advise their sales representatives on ways to improve sales performance.

They analyze sales statistics gathered by their staffs to determine sales potential and monitor the preferences of customers. Such information is vital to fine-tuning services and maximizing profits.

Promotion Managers

Promotion managers supervise staffs of promotion specialists. They direct promotion programs combining advertising with purchase incentives to increase sales of services. In an effort to establish closer contact with potential members or clients, promotion managers may be involved with direct mail, telemarketing, television or radio advertising, inserts in newspapers, and special events.

Member Services

This department is responsible for the day-to-day operations of meeting the members' needs and would include filing, data entry, incoming phone work, and related duties. Counselors or member representatives interview and enroll new members.

Telemarketers

Telemarketers are responsible for contacting potential members by phone to recruit new business.

Qualifications and Training

A wide range of educational backgrounds are suitable for entry into the dating service industry. Sales and customer representatives are sometimes expected to have some prior related experience, but many services are willing to train new graduates to the individual company's specific needs.

For management positions, some employers prefer a bachelor's or master's degree in business administration with an emphasis on marketing. Courses in business law, economics, accounting, finance, mathematics, and statistics are also highly recommended. However, many dating services value previous successful sales experience over formal degrees.

Most management positions are filled by promoting experienced staff or related professional personnel such as sales representatives. In small firms, where the number of positions is limited, advancement to a management position may come slowly. In large firms, promotion may occur more quickly.

Earnings

As in most sales-related fields, the income you can expect depends upon the level of your performance. Typically, dating service employees are paid on a commission basis or commission plus salary. For those on a strict commission basis, it means the more members they enroll, the more money they will make.

In addition, the higher the membership fee, the higher the income will be. Garry Hickerson, director of Great Expectations (and interviewed later in this chapter), reports that at his video dating service, salespeople in each department can make anywhere from $20,000 to $50,000 per year, depending upon their sales performance. The breakdown at Great Expectations for the different departments is as follows:

• Member services: 90 percent salary

• Sales and telemarketers: 70 percent commission (if they do well)

• Directors: base salary of $30,000 to $40,000 with a potential to make another $20,000 to $30,000 in commissions and bonuses.

Other types of services, such as computer on-line databases discussed earlier in this chapter will bring in earnings through sponsors or advertising.

Do You Have What It Takes?

More than intuitive matchmaking powers, in the professional dating service industry, job candidates need strong sales skills. Garry Hickerson gives this advice: "Make no mistake about it, this is first and foremost a sales-driven industry. People wishing to be successful in this industry should posses the ability to create an enthusiastic sales presentation. They must also have strong closing skills. I have found that people coming from the fitness, weight loss, time share, and travel sales fields seem to be somewhat more successful than those coming from a more conventional retail sales background."

For all of the dating service job positions named earlier, strong people skills is a must. In addition, managers and directors must possess the same skills found in any industry—the ability to organize and lead a group of people toward a similar goal; the ability to train and to supervise; an understanding of budgeting and finance; as well as an understanding of public relations and marketing skills.

People interested in becoming managers should be mature, creative, highly motivated, resistant to stress, and flexible yet decisive. The ability to communicate persuasively, both orally and in writing, with other managers, staff, and the public is vital.

Managers also need tact, good judgment, and exceptional ability to establish and maintain effective personal relationships with supervisory and professional staff members.

What It's Really Like

Garry Hickerson, Center Director, Great Expectations

Garry Hickerson has worked for Great Expectations, a video dating service, since 1996. The service has fifty centers across the United States; twelve are owned by individuals, and the other thirty-eight are owned by a private corporation. The centers are a combination of storefronts as well as office suites located inside of office complexes; Garry's center is located inside the Mobilecom building in Schaumburg, Illinois. You can access the website at http://www.great.expectations.com.

"If anyone had told me two years ago that I would end up working in the video dating industry, I would have had a good laugh," said Garry. "In April of '96, I was a general manager for one of the largest health club organizations in the world and was experiencing a very satisfactory growth and advancement track, when I was contacted by a headhunter about an opportunity in a 'similar industry.' It seems even headhunters are somewhat nervous about the stigma attached to the video dating industry. I'll never know what really prompted me to go to the initial interview (even my wife thought I was crazy). Perhaps I was reaching burnout in the fitness industry and didn't really know it. The first thing that struck me when I went into the center was the professionalism—not only the employees that I met that day, but also the environment of the center itself. Now that my interest was peaked, I found that all of the years of service and sales management that I had accumulated was a perfect fit for the singles industry. I was also offered a location five minutes from my home (I had been commuting for one hour), a very attractive compensation plan, and, perhaps most important, full autonomy over the center. After relating all of these benefits to my wife, her response was, 'When do you start?'"

Romance = Sales

"You have to be able to accept the challenge of reaching a monthly sales goal; foresee, respond, and cater to the needs of two thousand members; as well as recruit, train, and motivate a staff of ten to fifteen employees.

"As in any business, you will only be as good as the people who you hire and retain. There is not an abundance of employees that will walk into your door with experience in the industry, so it is very important to look for people who possess a high degree of confidence as well as solid sales, service, or telemarketing skills.

"My job is to take their existing skills and show them how to use them in this industry. This industry is a never-ending cycle of contacting people who have responded to direct mail, convincing them to come into the center to look at our programs, showing them how our programs would be beneficial to them, then providing them with the programs and service that they expect so that we can afford to send out more direct mail to recruit new members."

How It All Works

"First, you must realize that at Great Expectations we do not introduce or really 'matchmake' couples. Our organization is based upon the freedom of our members to choose who they wish to meet or if they wish to meet a particular person at all. Our members select each other based upon written information, pictures, and videos. Only when the member who has been selected gives mutual consent do we give out last names and phone numbers. It is then up to the members to decide who calls whom.

"One of the neatest stories that has come out of the Schaumburg center since I have been the director is about a couple that I will call Tom and Lisa. When Tom came to our center, he made the most insane video that we had ever seen. I mean this guy was nuts! He began his interview with a Tim Allen impersonation complete with power tools. Then he changed shirts and became a nose-picking nerd. From there he donned a lab coat, stethoscope, and wig and became a computer doctor, then Superman, and finally, a Hawaiian shirt and ukulele, while he sang 'you are so beautiful.'

"When we all watched the video (and believe me, we ALL did!), we were puzzled at first, but, after all, it was his membership. Even though he did get a lot of 'no, thank you' responses, he did finally meet Lisa, and they are now engaged. The moral of the story? He wanted someone who appreciated his sense of humor, not his millions of dollars!"

Staff Training

"The first training, no matter which position, is helping our employees understand the mind-set of our members and potential members. I believe that this industry does carry a certain stigma, and it is my job to teach my employees preventative professionalism (my term).

"Every member has a goal, whether it is marriage, steady relationship, or just to date a lot, and that goal is very important to them. Unfortunately, not every member reaches that goal during the initial membership, and the difference between renewing the membership or not often depends upon how they were treated.

"As far as job training, overcoming objections is priority one. Telemarketers must be able to overcome price objections in order to get a potential member to set an appointment (we do not give prices over the phone). Salespeople must be able to overcome procrastination objections during an interview. This training is ongoing—we never stop. Period. When a potential member comes through our door, they are nervous, frightened, and somewhat skeptical, but they also have a need. It is our job to convince them that their chances of meeting that need are much greater in our organization than the conventional avenues that they have been trying."

A Typical Day

"A typical day for me starts an hour before the center opens with a meeting with my member services manager. We discuss any member issues (yes, there are complaints—what business doesn't have them?), upcoming events for our members, and any changes in center or corporate policy that may be forthcoming.

"Following that, my attention turns to the appointments for sales for the day, meeting with my sales manager to discuss any staffing concerns during our busier hours (it's mostly an after 5 P.M. business), and any sales training topics that we feel need to be addressed.

"Finally, I meet with the telemarketing manager to ensure that our future appointments are set. Not bad for the first two hours of the day!

"Middays are somewhat slower: I use this time to answer any correspondence or return phone calls, and then I decide on a training topic for one of my departments and initiate a training session. We never stop trying to improve.

"After 5 P.M., it usually gets very busy, if you have recruited, hired, and trained your staff well, that is. This time is spent concentrating on the sales aspect of the business, and, hopefully, this is your most hectic time.

"The smoke clears around 9:30 or 10:00 P.M. You tally the day, send your reports to corporate, and go home. Busy? Yes. Hectic? Yes. Tiring? Yes. Disappointing? At times. Satisfying? Every time we enroll a new member! The greatest aspect about this business is the fact that we are here to try to improve the quality of life for our members. They are, for the most part, people who have good self-esteem and have decided to take a proactive step to try to satisfy their relationship goals, whether to date casually, find a serious relationship, or to get married or remarried, and there is no greater feeling than when a member fulfills that goal. I have personally seen this program work for all types of people, from millionaire business owners to handicapped convenience store employees."

The Upsides and Downsides

"Other than the satisfaction of seeing members successful with their goals, the best aspect of this job is the satisfaction of developing new employees. To me there are few things more rewarding than watching a new employee begin to reach his or her potential in this industry.

"Unfortunately, at times employees do not reach their potentials despite all of our combined efforts, and there comes a time when I have to make a decision for the best interest of the center—and that is probably the worst feeling that an employer ever has to face."

Some Advice for Getting Started

"Getting into this industry can be either easy or hard, depending upon the time of year and the needs of the center to which you apply.

"Avoid starting in December, a traditionally slow month, and always check with the Better Business Bureau before applying to any organization. It is also a good idea to find out how long the organization has been in business, how it recruits new members, how many members it enrolls each month, and how many potential members you can expect to see each day. When an organization is run well, it can be a very fun and rewarding career."

CHAPTER THREE

Say It with Words

M any creative romantics find an outlet for their talent through the written word. They are poets, love letter writers, and maybe even romance novelists. But is it possible to make a living, you might be wondering, committing romantic words to paper? For some, yes, but for most poets, for example, the answer is, sadly, no. Those poets who are able to find homes for their work often learn that the compensation is rarely more than a few dollars or a free copy of the publication in which their poetry has appeared. It is the rare exception who becomes well known—and financially comfortable—for his or her work. But then again, payment is not usually what spurs a writer to compose poetry. Satisfaction comes from crafting rhythmic lines, finding just the right word or metaphor to express themselves. Poetry is a balm for the soul, an outlet for the heart.

But there are other categories of romantic writers who are able to make a living doing something that they love. Read on to learn how to write romance novels for publication, start a love letter business, and even help other new romance writers get started.

Writing Romance Novels

Romance writers are creative, imaginative people. After all, they have to be; they make up stories for a living. Whether writing short stories or full-length novels, romance writers have to be able to create imaginary characters and events and make them seem real to their readers.

Romance writers have to be troublemakers, too, inventing all sorts of conflicts and problems for their characters. They have to make their conversations and thoughts entertaining, and fill their characters' lives with action. Finally, romance writers have to be expert problem solvers, helping their heroines find satisfying solutions to their troubles by the end of the story.

If you love to read romance and you find yourself stopping in the middle of a book and saying out loud, "I could do that better," then maybe you can.

Romance Industry Statistics

The following data has been compiled by the Romance Writers of America. (You will find more information about this important writers association later in this chapter.)

Romance Readers

- Romance readers range in age from eighteen to eighty-two.

- The average romance reader is thirty-nine.

- Forty-five percent of romance readers are college educated.

- More than 50 percent of romance readers work outside the home. Average household income is $40,000. (*Forbes*) Women who read romance novels make love with their partners 74 percent more often than do nonreaders. (*Psychology Today*)

The Romance Industry

- Popular fiction accounts for 91 percent of all mass-market book sales. Of all mass market book sales, 48.6 percent are romance novels.

- The all-time biggest seller in *Publishers Weekly* Bestsellers Fiction List was a romance novel. Book advances range from $500 to $5,000 for a first book.

Getting Started with Romance

The first thing you have to do as a potential romance writer is familiarize yourself with the different romance categories and decide where you might fit in. Romance is divided into two main categories—historical and contemporary. Within each of these there are further subcategories. A historical romance will cover a specific time period, such as Regency or Gothic. Contemporary romances can range from "sweet" to "sensuous." There are also romantic suspense novels, mainstream romances, and a category called "time travel romance," whose plots span both the historical and contemporary time periods. In addition, there are single-title romances and series romances.

Reading one or two romance novels, then deciding to give it a go, will not guarantee you much more than a lot of frustrating time wasted. You need to read not six but sixty romance novels. Go to the library or browse used book stores and pick up enough books representative of the different subcategories to give you an idea of what is being published. In addition, send a self-addressed, stamped envelope (SASE) to romance publishers (e.g., Silhouette, Harlequin, Avon, Zebra, etc.) and ask for their guidelines. Through these guidelines you will learn about the different lines and the requirements for each. To find romance publishers, check out the title pages of the novels you have picked up and also obtain a copy of a market guide (listed in Appendix B), which will give you more information covering what each publisher requires.

After you have read all those romance novels, it would be a good idea to read them again. But this time, instead of reading just for the story and your own enjoyment, go back and analyze each author's strengths and weakness. Study the books for characterization, dialogue, and plot. Identify the main conflict and read for pacing and suspense. It is not enough to craft a "boy meets girl" situation. There must be a reason for their meeting, something that brings them together, momentarily pulls them apart, and then ultimately allows them to resolve their problems and end up together. Yes, together. A romance novel must have a happy ending.

So, you have done all your reading, and now it's time to get down to the writing. Will you be able to give up your day job to do so? Read on.

The Writer's Life

Few new romance writers have the luxury of working at their craft full-time. Most need to maintain some other sort of employment to help pay the bills until they are able to support themselves through writing. Because of this, dedicated writers use every spare minute they have to work on their books or stories.

Writers who also have a full-time job get up an hour earlier, stay up an hour later, turn down invitations to parties or other social events, or let the housework go—whatever they can do to find the time to write.

Successful authors who support themselves through their writing treat it as a full-time job. Most report learning how to discipline themselves to put in a certain number of hours each day.

Every writer chooses a schedule with which he or she (yes, most romance writers are female, but there are a few men writing romance out there, too) can be comfortable. Some work in the early hours of the morning, take afternoon naps, then go back to the computer in the evenings. Others write for eight or ten or twelve hours straight each day for a period of months until the book is finished. Still others might take years to complete one volume.

There is no set formula for how a writer should work. The only rule is that you have to write. Author James Clavell said that even if you write only one page every day for a year, at the end of that time you'll have 365 pages. And that's a good-sized book.

Learning How to Write

For some, the craft of fiction comes naturally. It is an innate talent. For others, it is a craft they can learn. Rare is the new writer who turns out a first draft that meets a high enough standard to merit publication. New writers join critique groups, take writing classes, or pay professional critiquers to comment on their manuscripts' strengths and weaknesses. In the end, one of the best ways to achieve a high degree of competence is by reading how others do it, absorbing their techniques, then developing your own style. Writing is hard work. It takes time and persistence.

But say you have taken that time and shown that persistence, and your romance novel is finally done. Now what? Read on.

How to Get Published

Writing a short story or a full-length novel is only half the battle. In addition to honing your skills as an expert storyteller, you also have to be a knowledgeable salesperson. That means you must learn which publishers you should approach and how to approach them. There are several market guides, which are mentioned in Appendix B, that will tell you what categories of fiction the different publishers buy. The guides will also list the different magazines that purchase short stories. You can also check your own book collection to become more familiar with the publishers.

Once you've made a list of possible markets, you need to make sure your approach is appropriate. Your manuscript needs to be typed and double spaced, with your name at the top of each page. There are several sources that can give you the information you need to format your manuscript properly.

Before you send in your completed manuscript, you should write the editor a brief, usually one-page query letter describing your project. Include a one-page synopsis, or summary of your book's plot, and the first three chapters of your book as a sample. Don't forget to enclose an SASE, a self-addressed stamped envelope. The editor will use this to send you a reply. If the editor likes what he or she sees so far, you'll probably receive a request to send more.

Alternatively, you can look for an agent first, following the same steps you'd use to make your initial approach to a publisher. But this time, you are asking that the agent consider you as a possible client. At this point, after the query letters and sample chapters are in the mail, many new writers just sit back and wait for responses. The smart writer puts that manuscript out of her head and gets to work on the next one. And the next one. And the next one.

In the end, the key to getting published can be summed up in one word: persistence.

The Rewards, the Pay, the Perks

"Don't give up your day job just yet," is what the experts advise. Even if you manage to break in and sell your first novel, you would expect to receive only from about $500 to $5000.

The six-figure advances that some superstar authors receive are not the norm. Zebra Books senior editor John Scognamiglio says, "That kind of stuff like with John Grisham doesn't really have anything to do with the rest of us. There are 110,000 new titles a year, and there are only fifteen on the *New York Times* Best Sellers List at a time. Most of the rest of us are going to make a moderate income and do a civilized business if we work very, very hard. There's not that much room at the top. And there isn't much of a middle class in publishing. You either make a little bit of money, which the grand majority will do, or you make a lot."

If you do manage to land that first book contract, you will receive an advance against royalties. A royalty is a percentage, usually 6 to 10 percent, of the money your book earns in sales. The advance is often paid half on signing the contract, half on deliverance and acceptance of the manuscript.

But money is not the only reason writers write. For some, the profession is almost an obsession—a burning desire to put words to paper, to start a book and see it to its finish. They wouldn't be happy doing anything else.

Other perks include recognition and publicity, though some might view the attention as a downside.

Many writers report that the nicest perk is being able to go to work in a bathrobe.

What It's Really Like

Robyn Carr, Novelist

Robyn Carr has written fourteen books since 1980, most in the historical romance or category romance genre. She also recently switched genres, and her latest book, *Mind Tryst*, is an excellent psychological suspense/woman-in-jeopardy thriller published by St. Martin's Press. Robyn also taught for the Writer's Digest School of Writing and is the author of *Practical Tips for Writing Popular Fiction* (Writer's Digest Books).

How Robyn Got Started

"I'm a very ordinary person. I've been married for years, I have a couple of kids—until recently I even drove a station wagon. While I was pregnant, I read a lot and thought anybody with half a brain could do this, which is how everyone thinks in the beginning. You write that first book, and you're sure it's going to be *Gone with the Wind*, but it's really junk. But something happens to you when you're doing it. It held my interest to the point that it became an obsessive desire to write. I couldn't wait to get back to it.

"My first agent lived in San Antonio. He'd just opened the agency and was trying to build it up. He was my fourth or fifth attempt. I had been submitting things on my own before. I wrote query letters and killed myself hammering out synopses and revising the first three chapters four hundred times. I would get the envelope ready for the next submission before the rejection came so I wouldn't be paralyzed with grief.

"My agent made multiple copies and sent it to thirteen publishers—the thirteenth publisher took it. Avon, Bantam, and Berkley rejected it and my heart was sinking lower and lower. I knew there was no hope, then Little, Brown & Company finally bought it and I said Little who? They are one of the finest publishers in America but I hadn't heard of them.

"My first novel, *Chelynne*, was published in 1980. My first seven novels were historical romances, emphasis on history, published in hardcover (and therefore probably still available in the library) by Little, Brown & Company. They are *Chelynne*, *The Blue Falcon*, *The Bellerose Bargain*, *The Braiswood Tapestry*, *The Troubadour's Romance*, *By Right of Arms* (winner of the 1986 Rita Award), and *The Everlasting Covenant*.

"I also wrote some contemporary paperback romances from 1987 to 1989: *Tempted* (Bantam), *Informed Risk* (Silhouette), *Backward Glance* (Silhouette); one historical paperback (*Rogue's Lady*); and one family saga, hardcover (*Woman's Own*).

"I chose historical romance in the beginning because that's what I was reading. I was attracted to this genre by such books as *Katherine* by Anya Seton, *I Speak No Treason* by Rosemary Hawley Jarman, and some early King Arthur books. King Arthur is myth, but the others are actually based on well-known historical figures—Katherine Swynford, who married John of Gaunt and seeded a dynasty of English kings, and King Edward IV and Richard III.

"So, it was the romance of the history itself that intrigued me and it was from history that I got most of my ideas. I don't think romance writers get any more of a 'fix' from writing romance (rather than from real life) than suspense writers get a 'murder fix' from writing suspense—which implies people would either be 'doing it' or 'writing it.' This is not the case. People write because they love writing—and they are smart to choose a subject or genre in which they have enjoyed reading."

The Attraction of Romance

"Readers tend to love romance because if the novel is successful, it makes you feel romantic. In love. A passion or desire growing within you as you read, a vicarious feeling that is a product of the story of growing love between the hero and heroine.

"I guess that's what makes romance a good read—if it produces that emotional connection for the reader. And romances come in all shapes and sizes, from the chaste and pure little love stories that end with a first kiss to those sizzling and tempestuous romances filled with graphic sex. This is not only how readers choose their favorite types of romances, but also how writers choose what they will write.

"Writers generally use pen names if they don't want to be confused with anyone else or if they don't want to confuse their readers when they write for more than one genre or want to try something different from what they're known for."

The Writing Process

"I was on a panel at a writer's conference, and someone who wanted to write a book stood up and asked, 'What should you do? Should you force yourself to write the book from beginning to end, should you outline first, should you revise as you go along?' Everyone on the panel of six published authors—and some of them were very successful and making tons and tons of money—said that you should really outline first and force yourself to write through and then revise. However, I keep getting stuck going back to the beginning and revising and revising before I can carry on.

"I have a very clear idea before I begin what's going to happen. Some minor things change but the basic premise—who the hero is and how it's going to end—is real solid. I can't get past fifty pages without revising twenty times, and then I can't get past a hundred pages without revising twenty times, and when I really hit my stride and the momentum takes me through to the end is at about three hundred pages."

Developing Characters

"Until I've written an entire book I'm not clear on what my characters' personalities are and how they feel about things. I'm always too passive in the first draft, reluctant to say someone is so fat Omar the Tent Maker has to make her gown. I'll say that she's overweight or she's a little on the chubby side. Or I give people emotions, like *uncomfortable*—passive stuff—until I can finally get down and dirty about how they really feel. They're either angry or they're not, they're either scared or they're not—but they're not uncomfortable.

"Another problem is the expression 'she felt numb,' or 'she didn't know how she felt,' which usually means I don't know what she's feeling. But that won't work in fiction. The personality has to be clearly defined."

Earnings

"The income for romance writers varies so greatly, it almost isn't worth mentioning. Kensington is buying sixty-thousand-word romances for a new line of theirs and paying a $500 flat fee, no royalties. On the other hand, there are *New York Times* bestselling authors earning millions a year. Unfortunately, there is no 'average income' to report. It always has been and always will be difficult to work as a paid novelist—the competition is fierce and the marketplace is fickle."

Advice from Robyn Carr

"As a serious writer, you can better your chances of breaking into the field by a) reading in the genre you wish to write—reading voraciously; b) studying writing through classes, conferences, how-to books, and critique groups; c) being prepared to market aggressively and weather rejection, which is the nature of the business; and d) doing more actual writing than anything else.

"The best advice I can give a beginning novelist is to be absolutely sure you are writing what you like to read. If you read mostly romances, don't attempt to write a mainstream coming-of-age fiction; likewise, if you are reading mostly mystery, don't try to write a romance because you think it will be easier or your chances of publishing will be better. Whatever book keeps you awake at night—try to write that kind of book."

Romantics Helping Romantics

If you are a writer with a talent for editing and/or teaching, you can create a career for yourself helping other writers get started. New writers just starting out sometimes feel as if they are working in a vacuum; they don't know where to turn for feedback and advice. Often they fall prey to the many unscrupulous people out there, trying to make money from the dreams and concerns of new writers. Some of them pose as agents and offer a critiquing service. The implication is that a writer will be represented after paying high reading and/or critiquing fees. But this rarely happens. Talented critiquers, though, with no hidden agenda can carve out a successful niche for themselves.

Starting a Critiquing Service

If you are a good writer yourself, you have a talent for spotting the flaws that often mar a new writer's manuscript, and you know how to point out those flaws in a constructive manner, you have the skills needed to offer a critiquing service. The first step is to let other people know about your service. Advertising in publications read by writers, *Writer's Digest* magazine, for example, or contacting writing groups such as the local chapter of Romance Writers of America is a good place to start. After a few happy clients, word of mouth will also help spread the word, and the referrals will start coming in.

Pricing Your Services

Fees charged by critiquers usually run from $1.40 to as high as $5.00 a page, although the latter amount is deemed excessive by most. You need to see how long it takes you to critique a full manuscript, including making margin notes and writing up your report, to accurately assess the amount you need to charge. Manuscripts are usually mailed to you by clients, and if you instruct them so, they will include a self-addressed stamped mailer for the return of their work. This will save you having to take the cost of postage and return envelopes into account. You are mainly charging for your time and your expertise. It is up to you to decide what hourly rate you need to earn.

Teaching Writers to Write

There are many opportunities and settings to teach others to write. In some situations, such as at the college level, you will need a master's or even a Ph.D. degree to qualify. In other settings, such as evening adult education classes, your own proven track record as a writer will be enough to get you in the door. You can also plan and organize novel writing seminars and workshops on your own and advertise your services locally.

Still another avenue for teaching writers is to work for the many on-line services that offer self-enrichment courses.

America Online is one such service with an Online Campus that has an extensive English and Writing Department. You have to subscribe to AOL to be able to teach there, but their new rate plan offers a low monthly fee (which is waived for instructors) and unlimited on-line hours. In addition, instructors are paid a base fee per each registered student, between $15.00 and $32.50, depending upon the length of your class. To learn more about AOL's Online Campus, use the keyword "Classes."

One such innovative AOL course offered at this writing is called Write Like a Lover! Workshop, taught by Tad Wojnicki.

What It's Really Like

Tad Wojnicki, Author and Instructor

Tad Wojnicki wants every workshop participant to open up to "free writing, mad play, intuitive and sensual exploration of the world." He wants everyone to write like a lover!

"When I talk about my students' writing, I never use the word 'bad.' Any writing that has come from a living and breathing soul is good. Because of that I use—and encourage everybody to use—just two questions while critiquing any written work:

1. What is in your writing that makes you feel something, that creates an involuntary response somewhere in your body?

2. How could it be enhanced?"

Tad Wojnicki is the author of the novel, *Lie Under the Fig Trees* (Edward R. Smallwood, Inc., 1996), an exotic, brooding tale of crazy love, betrayal, and redemption set against the lush, heady paradise of the Mexican tropics.

Like Teddy, the hero of *Lie Under the Fig Trees*, Tad writes a lot of love letters. "I have written thousands of them over the years," Tad admits, "using café napkins, bar bills, pizza flyers, and scratch paper I found in Kinko's trash cans. What became apparent to me is that I could quickly splash some ink on paper and create a sharp, engaging, vivid letter, able to leave a lasting impression on the reader."

Also like Teddy, Tad first wrote to woo. "I was sitting at the Renaissance Café in Berkeley, sipping my beloved café au lait, licking the softly bitter, puffy milk foam from my lips, wretchedly alone and lonely, writing for love. Writing up a storm. Scribbling to one of my pen pals, I decided I would write in such a loving, vivid, knee-weakening way that she would fall in love with me. She did. And that's what the best writing is like in any of the creative writing workshops I teach."

While firing out tons of love letters, Tad tried to write serious fiction. Somehow, though, he couldn't get past the first few words. "The first words got me stuck. Why? I would open my squeaky-clean notebook, finger the slick pages, touch the warm lines, write a sentence, and then I'd keep stroking the sentence— till it was dead. Madly bent on absolute perfection, I felt I couldn't go ahead unless the first sentence was just so. I was stuck.

"Finally, one beautiful day, I saw the paradox. Why is it I can fire out a terrific love letter any time I want, I kept asking myself aloud, staggering like a drunk around the UC campus until midnight. In the morning, I threw my notebook containing my perfectionist, unfinished sentences away, and, with my hand already itching to scrawl, scrawl I did, whatever I felt like, without watching the lines, all over the page.

"Soon, I started writing for money, and I started writing to prove myself, to see whether anybody would buy what I wrote. First fillers, small pieces, then short stories, and finally the daddy of them all, a novel. I sold them all."

Tad Wojnicki's Background

Tad was born in Poland and made the transition into the English language upon his arrival in the United States in 1977. His poems and short stories have appeared in the *Baltimore Sun, Porter Gulch Review, Leviathan, The Real World Press, Midstream: A Jewish Review, Llano Estacado Review,* and other magazines.

Tad received a Ph.D. in Biblical Studies from the Catholic University of Lublin, Poland, and an M.F.A. in Creative Writing from San Francisco State University.

"In Berkeley, California, I started my own little magazine named *Kontakty (Contacts)* together with a few other Polish immigrants. The magazine made no money, really, but it was fun to write, edit, and self-publish. While publishing *Kontakty,* I worked in a print shop, still writing in Polish. I didn't feel I could express a feeling in English—and that, to me, was a must if I wanted to jump from one language to another.

"In 1982, I was hired to teach the Polish language at the Defense Language Institute in Monterey, California. This day job made it possible for me to travel to Europe, Africa, even around the globe, and to do a lot of writing. In 1985, I felt confident enough about my English to start recording my feelings in the language and then, in 1989, to quit the comfort of a government job in order to think, write, speak, and dream only in English."

Since 1992, Tad has taught his Write Like a Lover! Workshop (in addition to in his on-line classroom) at the Hartnell College in Salinas, California, and recently at the Mendocino Coast Writers' Conference. He now lives in Carmel, California, where he organizes the bohemian beach parties known as "poetry pow-wows," attended by the local literati calling themselves The Angels by the Sea. "The village of 'Carmel-by-the-Sea' had a tradition of bohemian clambakes. The early bohemians included George Sterling, Mary Austin, Sinclair Lewis, and Jack London. But they are dead. With their deaths, the clambakes died, too. The present-day Carmel literati has brought the tradition back to life. Every month, rain or shine, we gather by the beach fire singing, performing poetry, telling tales, attracting guests from near and far. Where there's fire, there's smoke."

Tad Wojnicki also has a manuscript critique service, offering criticism, career guidance, and marketing tips.

The Writer's Life

"I've chosen a risky, bumpy business, full of pitfalls, rip-offs, and with no guarantees whatsoever of any payoff during a lifetime. Being an artist is the art of living dangerously.

"The big thing about being a writer is that you carry your business wherever you go. You work your own hours, which means, of course, you work all the time—at the restaurant table, eaves-dropping on your neighbors' conversations, at any odd job you take to survive, while shopping, while chatting on the phone, while kneading dough, even while *haciendo amor*. But since you love your work, you feel you are the luckiest dog alive. 'The writer's life may be a dog's life,' Anatole France said, 'but it is the only life worth living.'

"The teaching is a part of my being a writer. I love to teach, and I don't think I would ever give up my teaching, even if I strike it big. Being a writer, to me, equals being a rabbi, a teacher of life."

Advice from Tad Wojnicki

"Unfortunately, too many writers create their books but don't create their lives. They become senseless drunks, couch potatoes, or dried-up forget-me-nots. In my opinion, every writer should be a star, beautiful in and out. He or she should live a life as spectacular and worth telling as that of a race car driver or a football player, showing the reader the way. I see the writer as a lifestyle guru.

"To be romantic is to strike a lifestyle by one's own blueprint. It means creating self-styled events, self-styled relationships, self-styled growth as an individual—that is, to create self-styled ways to happiness. Your lifestyle blueprint must match your fingerprints. Whatever you do must be true to yourself.

"What's the ultimate reward of being true to yourself? The feeling of being free. The wind in your hair is romantic! So make things happen, instead of letting things happen to you."

Tad Wojnicki is a member of the National Writers Union, the California Writers Club, and is listed in *A Directory of American Poets and Fiction Writers, 1997–1999*.

Starting a Love Letter Writing Service

Can you write love letters as Tad Wojnicki does, from the heart, from the soul, letters that create for their readers a knee-weakening reaction? If so, then consider starting your own letter writing service. Who would use this service? Other romantics, of course, but those who cannot express themselves in words the way they'd like.

Advertise your services locally, in the newspaper or singles' magazines. Go to clubs, the beach, resorts, or wherever else romantic souls congregate and pass your flyer or business card around. Word of mouth will soon have you on your way to a successful career.

Romance Writers of America

The Romance Writers of America, founded in 1980, is a national, nonprofit organization dedicated to promoting excellence in the romance writing field. To date, more than five thousand people are members of RWA.

The benefits this organization offers to new writers are extensive. Through both the national conference and local chapters, writers can find their peers, share concerns and ideas, and network with professionals in the field, including published authors, agents, and editors.

RWA members receive *Romance Writers Report*, a bimonthly magazine that includes marketing information, contest and conference listings, "how-to" articles written by experts, and free promotion for members' books.

RWA gives out an annual Rita Award to honor excellence in published novels in various categories. Author Robyn Carr (featured earlier in this chapter) was a Rita Award recipient.

RWA also holds the annual Golden Heart Writing Competition. This contest provides opportunities for the manuscripts of unpublished writers to come to the attention of editors and agents. Many published romance writers credit their first sales to this prestigious competition. Local chapters also hold writing contests that give valuable guidance to writers.

The annual national conference and the annual conferences of many local chapters provide settings for new and seasoned writers to meet and learn. Conference activities include workshops, one-on-one appointments with agents and editors, roundtable discussions, book-signing events, and hundreds of informal networking opportunities.

To find out more about RWA and the local chapter nearest you, contact the national RWA office. The address is provided in Appendix A.

More Advice for Romance Writers

1. Don't be afraid of criticism; part of writing is rejection.

2. Don't get too attached to your words. Writing shouldn't be called "writing" at all; the better name for it is "rewriting," because that's what all writers must constantly do.

3. Whatever you submit should be professionally presented. It should be neatly typed, with margins and a nice cover letter. The presentation is what first catches an editor's or agent's eye.

4. Keep writing. Don't ever stop trying to perfect your skills.

5. And don't give up. If you do, it's guaranteed that you won't get published. If you keep at it, you'll eventually find a home for your work.

For More Information

Related professional associations and reading resources are provided for you in Appendixes A and B.

CHAPTER FOUR

Say It with Flowers

A delivery truck pulls up into the driveway, your doorbell rings, and suddenly you are confronted with a beautiful, fragrant arrangement of fresh flowers. Isn't it exciting? Who sent them? What a romantic or warm, friendly gesture. Indeed, who wouldn't be thrilled at being on the receiving end of such a lovely gift?

For romantics, making that excitement happen could be the ideal career for you. If working with flowers interests you, there are many options to pursue.

"Say it with flowers" was a campaign slogan the Society of American Florists coined and publicized in a million dollar advertising campaign begun in 1924. Since that time, millions of consumers have been doing just that—saying it with flowers—on Mother's Day and Valentine's Day, at senior proms and on graduation day, at weddings and churches, at hospitals and funerals, at dinner parties and elegant society balls. But without floral professionals, we wouldn't have much to say it with.

Floriculture as a Career

The art and science of floriculture can be viewed as a series of stages. First the flowers must be grown and tended, then made available to retailers. Before the customer can have an order filled, the flowers must be tended to again, made into creative arrangements or placed in strategic locations within the home or office.

The options include growing, importing, wholesaling and brokering, retailing, and designing.

Growing Plants

Growers start the beginning of the process and in many ways perform the most crucial function in the chain. Without the expertise and care of experienced growers, there would be no flowers to market to the general public.

Growers deal with the basics: they plants bulbs or seeds in the ground and raise them to sell as cut flowers. Their customers are wholesalers or brokers or retailer florists and nursery owners.

Although many cut flowers available for sale in the United States are grown in other countries (see "Importers" later in this chapter), U.S. growers can still flourish here on native soil.

What It's Really Like

Barry Brand, Grower

As Barry Brand, a grower based in Carpinteria, California, explains it, "Most of the flowers grown in other countries are roses and carnations and chrysanthemums. But we don't grow those. I looked for different niches in the marketplace, and I grow flowers that are difficult to grow. As long as you do it well, you can be successful."

Barry owns three different farms with more than one hundred acres. Some of his land supports greenhouses and shade houses (structures that protect the flowers from the sun). The largest amount of acreage is devoted to field flowers.

He grows a variety of crops, including lilies, freesias, tulips, gerbera, delphinium, larkspur, snapdragons, sunflowers, and alstroemeria. He reports that business is booming—to the tune of $5 million dollars worth, in fact. Each year, millions and millions of stems (the way flowers are counted) go from Barry's farms to market.

Job Titles in Cut-Flower Growing

Running a big operation like Barry's requires a healthy number of workers. Barry has about seventy-four employees. The job titles found in cut-flower growing include:

- *Field workers:* As the job title implies, field workers are found in the field taking care of the different crops. They plant and weed and pick the flowers when they are ready for market.

- *Overseers:* Each crop has its own overseer who manages the field workers. The overseer is responsible for all the daily care the flowers need.

- *Production managers:* Production managers report back to the head grower or owner and keep track of all the different crops. They are responsible for overall production, including taking care of fertilizing and pesticide spraying schedules.

- *Graders:* The graders sort through the flowers, dividing them into bunches in three different groups based on quality.

- *Salespeople:* The salespeople contact wholesalers and retailers across the country, letting them know what crops are available for sale.

- *Data entry and office workers:* The office staff takes care of computerizing sales information and all the other administrative tasks involved with running a cut-flower farm.

- *Warehouse staff:* The warehouse staff takes care of the flowers when they come in from the field and get them ready to go out to market. Staff members supervise the coolers and are responsible for packing the flowers in boxes for shipping.

How Barry Brand Got His Start

Barry grew up in Holland, where he completed a three-year course in floriculture. "My father was a grower in Holland and the original plan was for me to become a partner with him, but I wanted to see the United States before I did that. After I visited here, I decided to stay."

That was in 1985. During his first year here, Barry worked for different nurseries, learning the ropes. Then his brother and father left Holland to join him in California. Barry and his brother started a small family nursery growing snapdragons, leasing the property rather than buying it. Every month their operation grew, and after one year their father joined them in partnership. By 1989, they had expanded so much that they split the nursery into two different operations, and Barry formed a new business partnership with his wife, who now works with him at their three California farms.

He now owns most of the land outright. Barry sums it up: "We started with nothing, and now we're doing pretty well."

The secret to his success? "I think we grow the right crops, and we put a lot of time into it. We also have the belief that we can do it. I always knew that I was going to be a flower grower. You don't take 'no' for an answer—you just have to believe in yourself."

Having a great love for what you do is also important. "I've always liked working with nature. Every day is different, a challenge. It's never boring."

What It Takes

Barry Brand's advice is for any potential grower to go to school. "Learn as much as you can about plants but also about business. Studying business in school was a big help to me. My wife, Wilja, who is also my partner, has a strong business background, too. This is probably why we're so successful.

"Also, before I started my own, I worked for a lot of other nurseries. You learn from how other people run their businesses. Even if you grew up on a farm, you should work for other people first, in any position you can, before you start out on your own.

I started as a field worker, then worked my way up to manager. You can't be afraid to work."

Importers

Most of the flowers that you'll order from a florist shop have not been grown domestically. Although some originate in Europe, in particular in Holland, most are imported to the United States from Central and South America. In general, costs are lower there, land is less expensive, and the climatic conditions are more favorable, saving the expense of heating greenhouses.

Importers coordinate all the various steps involved with bringing in flowers from growers or suppliers in other countries. They are responsible for the masses of paperwork necessary before the flowers can be shipped to the various wholesalers, brokers, or retail outlets. Some of the documentation includes plant inspections, plant quarantines, and customs.

What It's Really Like

Colleen Taber, Importer

Colleen Taber has been in the cut-flower import business for more than twenty years, and in the spring of 1994 she became the sole owner of her company, Gardens America. Most importers are based in southern Florida, and Colleen's sales office is in Pembroke Pines, near Miami. She also has a warehouse on a runway of Miami International Airport so flowers can go directly from the plane to the cooler.

Although most importers bring in flowers from a variety of different growers, Colleen works with only one supplier, Gardens of the Andes, which is based in Bogotá, Colombia. "I find if I give all of my attention to the one grower, that's what the grower gives back to me," Colleen explains. "Because of the relationship with the grower, I can tell them a year in advance what I need them to grow for me, what color varieties I need each week, what I need for a holiday, and I know that their only concern is me. We work that well together that I can send out promotional material to the customer, and they'll know that on week three, for example, they'll have pompoms and alstroemeria in the boxes; on week twenty-two, they'll have lilies, fujis, and carnations. There's never a guess."

Although Colleen works with only one grower, she in turn sells to more than three hundred customers in the United States. "I'm unique in the way I work," Colleen says. "I'm the only importer who sells strictly on a standing-order basis. That means that I call customers, or customers call me and say they would like to be a customer of Gardens America. I process their credit applications, and then I take their orders—which is for the same amount every week of the year. So the flowers come in here already sold. Other importers bring in the product and store it in the cooler while they're trying to sell it."

Colleen's Background

Colleen started in the business working for her parents, who were the original owners of Gardens America, and learned everything from the ground up. Her advice: "For everything you learn, you can learn two things by your mistakes. So I made sure I made plenty of mistakes. Not by choice, really, just by sheer lack of skill. But what I found is that with the world so competitive, it's much better to have some kind of formal training. We employ three full-time salespeople who sell to three hundred customers and do more than $21 million in sales each year. But my sales staff never really had any formal training. Recently, we all enrolled in a Dale Carnegie sales course, and we have seen a big difference."

Training for Importers

If you want to work as an importer, Colleen's suggestion is to try to get a job with an importer, doing whatever you can get hired to do. "You can never see a picture as clearly from the top as from the bottom," she says.

Alternatively, Colleen recommends finding work with a broker who handles all the paperwork that goes to U.S. Customs. "Or, get a job with U.S. Customs," Colleen suggests. "Then you can see what happens and what all the pitfalls are. You have to be very careful, especially when you're dealing with countries where there are strong drug implications. It's a real hardship for legitimate growers who have to go to extremes to make sure nothing gets into the boxes of flowers except flowers. And on this end, every single package is x-rayed and filmed. They even identify the packer; they initial each box. The precautions are very detailed."

Positions with an Importer

The number of staff varies with the size of each business. Colleen employs one assistant, three salespeople, one bookkeeper, one receptionist, one billing clerk, one statistician (who takes care of tracking all the sales figures), and four packers and shippers who handle all operations at her warehouse.

Earnings for an Importer

Salaries also vary from importer to importer. In general, however, salespeople can make the best living. Although some importers pay their staff on a commission (1.5 to 2.5 percent of collected sales) or commission plus salary basis, Colleen reports that her salespeople working with the standing-order accounts earn a set salary of approximately $52,000 per year.

And while warehouse staff who basically move boxes around might earn just above minimum wage for other importers, at

Gardens America they earn between $20,000 and $25,000 a year. "I do as well as I do with few people," Colleen explains, "because I pay them well and treat them well, and then they work better."

Brokers and Wholesalers

Brokers and wholesalers perform similar functions. They purchase stock directly from growers or importers and supply florists with fresh flowers, decorative plants, and other related items. However, how they work with the florists differs a great deal.

Based on the estimated need of their regular customers, wholesalers buy a certain quantity of flowers each week at a price determined by the growers or importers. This could be, for example, a thousand boxes of fresh carnations (with six hundred carnations to a box), five hundred cases of pompoms, and fifty dozen roses. At the beginning of the week, when the florists' coolers need replenishing and the wholesalers' stock is fresh, the wholesalers add in their expenses and set a profit to the price given to the florists. As the week goes by and the flowers are no longer in peak condition, the wholesaler will adjust the price downward, according to what the market can bear. The wholesaler's earning power can see a great deal of fluctuation.

Wholesalers receive their flowers from their suppliers, store them, usually in a refrigerated warehouse, provide them with any care and conditioning they need, then deliver them to the florists. The florists are usually located within an easy delivery distance from the wholesaler, most likely within a fifty-mile radius.

In addition to standing orders, wholesalers supply florists with special orders. They can send one rare bird-of-paradise or a half dozen orchids for a bride's bouquet. Brokers go directly to the grower or importer and get a price for a particular item. That price is set for the day and will not change. After adding the profit margin to the price, the broker then, usually over the telephone, sells the stock to the florists. Only after actually selling the flowers will the broker go back to the grower and plant down his money, so to speak.

This procedure, of selling stock at a guaranteed price, eliminates all risk for the broker. In addition, the broker is not responsible for warehousing and taking care of plants. He or she doesn't even have to get involved in shipping; the grower or importer can send the purchase overnight directly to the florist, who can be located anywhere in the country.

On the surface, considering the benefits to the broker, it is surprising that there are any wholesalers in business. They have all the financial risk and most of the responsibility of keeping the flowers in good condition. A broker needs only a telephone and a good sales pitch.

However, most retail florist shops prefer to work with local wholesalers. The florist can drop in, see what's in stock, and pick out a few of this and a few of that. Wholesalers will handle special orders or spur-of-the moment deliveries. Wholesalers will also give the florist a call every morning and ask what he or she needs. The order is then placed on the truck and arrives by the afternoon. Brokers are not equipped to do this.

The customers brokers deal with are usually large retail outlets that handle a large volume of business. They place orders on a weekly or twice weekly as opposed to a daily basis. Many florists work with both brokers and wholesalers. They get their day-to-day orders through the wholesaler and go to brokers to supplement that with the larger orders they know in advance they're regularly going to need. For example, a florist who regularly sells one hundred carnations a week will place that order through a broker. The other orders, such as for weddings or funerals, will go to the wholesaler.

What It's Really Like

Pat Reese, Broker

Pat Reese is a pioneer in the brokering business, having started as a broker fifteen years ago. "I'd like to think, though I can't prove this, that I was, if not the first, then at least the second broker in cut flowers. When I started, there really was no one else doing this. It was all by the traditional wholesaling method. Now, of course, there are quite a few brokers. And what has happened is that many of the growers have seen what a brokering business can do, and they have formed their own brokerage companies."

Pat Reese started out working with a floral publishing company as an advertising manager. He stayed with them for nine years, then went on to the flower-by-wire service business as a field representative with Teleflora. (You'll find more information about careers with wire services later in this chapter.) When he left Teleflora fifteen years ago to become a broker, he was vice president of sales in California.

"After having spent almost twenty years of my adult life being in and around florist shops, I kept seeing a need for a more efficient system. I was running into disgruntled florists all the time who were upset with their local wholesalers for a hundred different reasons. At the same time, the fax machine was just starting to make its way in, and transportation was something I'd always been interested in, and it became a desire to find a different way. I wanted to build a better mousetrap. And I did. I took my idea to three former presidents of Teleflora and each one of them became a full partner in my company, which is called Floral International Xpress, or FIX. I was the operating officer, and they were investors."

Since then, Pat has bought out his investors and is now sole proprietor.

What You'll Need to Become a Broker

Pat Reese suggests that the first thing you should do if you're interested in this kind of career is to make sure you know the flower industry. When he plunged in, he already knew thousands of florists on a first-name basis and had a ready-made list of customers.

You also have to have a good sales background, Pat advises, and, for brokering, you need telemarketing skills. Most, if not all, of your selling will be done over the telephone. You need to know about distribution and also have a strong financial background.

A source of start-up capital is also necessary for both brokering and wholesaling, although the amount is usually smaller for the new broker. Brokers don't have overhead to worry about or warehouses or refrigeration or insurance and employees and delivery. They can work anywhere they can install a telephone.

But for both professions, until you've established yourself with the growers and importers, you'll have to pay up front for the goods you purchase. There's always a gap of time before you get paid by the florists, and you have to be able to cover yourself during that period.

Florists

Florists either own and operate their own shops or work in a shop for someone else. There are three kinds of flower shops: cash-and-carry stores, decorator shops, and service shops.

Cash-and-carry stores, or merchandising stores as they are also known, sell bunches of prewrapped flowers. Generally, customers cannot order special arrangements through cash-and-carry shops; their selections are limited to what is immediately available and on hand. Cash-and-carry shops are found in the neighborhood supermarket's flower section, at farmers' markets, or at impromptu "shops" set up in buckets alongside of the road.

Decorator shops, which are few and far between, operate as specialists, custom making arrangements for important occasions such as weddings or balls. They generally do not cater to walk-in customers.

The largest percentage of florists are service florists, meaning they offer a service in addition to a product. They design and custom make and deliver the merchandise.

The jobs available in florist shops include owner, manager, salesperson, floral designer, delivery personnel, interior scaping and maintenance personnel.

Location, Location, Location

As with any business that hopes to garner off-the-street customers, location is always the first consideration. Because flowers are considered to be more a luxury item than a necessity (although fervent plant lovers would surely argue for the latter definition), most successful florist shops are found in suburban town centers as opposed to downtown locations. Florist shops can also do well in shopping malls.

The Skills You'll Need

To be a successful florist, a love of plants, although crucial, is not enough. Florists must have training in every aspect of the industry, including strong business skills. The best preparation is gaining a combination of on-the-job experience and education.

Trainees can gain experience working part-time for retail and wholesale florists, for greenhouses and nurseries, or for cut-flower growers. With this kind of exposure, potential florists can learn about packing and unpacking, processing, shipping, propagation, cutting, seed sowing, bulb planting and potting, the basics of floral design, and pickup, delivery, and sales work.

While in school, students should take courses in biological sciences, math, communications, computer science, and general business, including retail store management.

Some academic and vocational institutions offer two- and four-year programs geared directly to floriculture and horticulture. Many also provide students with the opportunity for training while in school through cooperative education programs. Co-op programs place students in related business settings and, after the first year of academics, alternate semesters with work and study.

The Society of American Florists has prepared a list of colleges, universities, and postsecondary schools offering two- and four-year degree programs and technical and certificate-awarding programs. The courses cover general horticulture, ornamental horticulture, floriculture and floral design. The Society's address can be found in Appendix A.

The Downsides of the Job

Florists work long hours and, as Al Mendoza, proprietor of Keepsake Flowers and Gifts in Dolton, Illinois, says, "When most people are out enjoying the various parties, you're working at them. During holiday times, most people are having fun, enjoying the festivities, but, again, it's the busiest time of the year for florists. In the floral world, you don't get weekends and holidays off. I can't remember the last time my family and I could share a decent holiday together. Christmas, Easter. You're working like crazy the week before, then you're so exhausted, you can't enjoy yourself." (Al Mendoza talks more about his work later in this chapter.)

The Finances

To start a florist shop these days, an initial investment of about $50,000 would be required. And in today's economy, Al says, you can expect to work eight to ten years before realizing a profit.

"It's a risk when you're dealing with perishables. A person could lose a lot if they don't know how to order. If they order too much they can lose, or if they don't order enough they can lose. A typical example would be Valentine's Day. If you order too many roses, if you buy a thousand too many, you can lose thousands of dollars. But it's hard to learn how to get the ordering right. That's why it's so important to work for other florists before venturing out on your own. You need the experience."

Retail Nurseries

Although some florists might occasionally grow their own plants to sell, most of the time they purchase their products from wholesalers or brokers. Nurseries, on the other hand, generally grow on-site most of the product they sell to the public.

What It's Really Like

Michael O'Donnell, O'Donnell Farms

Michael O'Donnell is proprietor of O'Donnell Farms, a wholesale and retail nursery and garden center in Coconut Creek, Florida. "Most of the things we sell we grow ourselves," Michael explains, "and there are certain things we buy. Nobody in this business raises everything. There are at least 1.8 million species of plants. We grow more than seven hundred different types of items here. But we're a bit unusual in that respect. Most nurseries grow only a dozen or so items."

O'Donnell Farms raises shade trees, a large selection of palms, bushes, ground covers, orchid plants, and house plants. Michael O'Donnell started out as a hobbyist and was actively involved in the American Orchid Society. In addition, he comes to the nursery field with many years experience in the business world. "I think it's very helpful to have a business background coupled with horticultural knowledge. You have to be familiar with production management, buying, selling, pricing, maintenance, care. This is like our own little world here. We have our own electrical and plumbing systems, we propagate plants from seed and stem cuttings and meristem tissue culture. We try to be self-sufficient."

Positions in a Nursery

Nurseries employ a wide range of personnel. O'Donnell Farms has a landscape designer; a landscape supervisor who oversees the outside jobs; a nursery supervisor who oversees the propagation of the plant material and directly manages the employees under him; field-workers who take care of growing all the plants; a maintenance overseer who keeps a large fleet of trucks, front loaders, and cranes in working operation; office staff (a secretary and bookkeeper); and a sales staff.

Training for Nursery Work

Sales staff, field-workers, and supervisors all must be knowledgeable about all aspects of both indoor and outdoor gardening, from soil conditions to fertilizers and pesticides.

They have to be familiar with all the different plants: where they come from, what they're called, how to grow them, how to take care of them.

Some education in horticulture is essential, as is hands-on training and on-the-job experience.

Earnings for Nursery Workers

Earnings can range from $5.50 through $10.00 an hour to $25,000 to $60,000 a year, depending on the position you land. Sales staff working on commissions and landscape designers and supervisors generally make the most money. A field worker caring for orchids might start out at a lower salary, but it would be possible to work up the ladder into management.

But if the salaries don't quite measure up, most dedicated plant lovers don't seem to mind. As Michael O'Donnell puts it, the attraction is "to work with living material, to watch something grow. It's like a call of nature. Some people are called to the sea, some people are called to the plant world. I've done everything I've wanted to do with my life—I wanted to be the president of a big company, and I've done that, and now I'm doing exactly what I want to do."

Wire Services

It's Valentine's Day, and a young man working in Seattle telephones or visits a local florist. He chooses a traditional dozen red roses (long stems) and has them sent to his financée, who is attending school in Boston, Massachusetts. He pays by credit card over the phone, or by credit card, check, or cash in person. The Seattle florist contacts a Boston shop, and, in no time, the young woman receives her Valentine's gift.

The Seattle florist took the order, arranged for the flowers, and collected the money. The Boston florist provided the flowers and had them delivered. But how does that shop receive payment? Through the wire services. There are six major wire services in the country (FTD, Teleflora, AFS, Florafax, Carik, and Redbook), and they act as clearinghouses for the financial transactions between participating florists around the country.

What It's Really Like

Charlene Dunn, American Floral Services

Charlene Dunn, vice president of marketing at AFS (American Floral Services), the largest of the wire services, explains, "When a florist sends an order to another state, for example, the florist on the sending side has the money; the florist on the receiving end has done most of the work. What we do is take the money from one and we give it to the other—assuring that payment is made to that person."

Jobs with a Wire Service

Wire services offer a range of positions—AFS, for example, employs approximately 160 people—falling into the following job titles: executive officers, financial officers, credit and state-ment clerks, human resource workers (personnel), operations workers, directory service workers (the people who publish the directories of participating florists), customer services, inter-national relay services, field staff, and educators.

Field staff are mainly marketing counselors whose job is to go from shop to shop offering help. They must have a sales back-ground and knowledge of the floral industry. "Partly what they do," Charlene explains, "is make sure that florists have what they need as far as the services we offer. In addition to the financial end of things, AFS is involved in other related activities. We have design and management training, educational publications, and computer software to improve the efficiency, profitability, and professionalism of AFS florists. We also help with marketing and provide point-of-purchase products, such as window posters and banners advertising various holiday arrangements."

Wire services employ field staff all over the country. When an opening comes up, they advertise it in the local newspaper in the area where they need to hire someone. The advertisements would usually be found under "sales."

"We also employ a large number of educators to help with pro-fessional floral development," says Charlene. "Thousands of florists from around the world have attended our education cen-ter. We offer programs in floral design, commentating, manage-ment, and computer skills. We also go out into the field and train florists across the country through our seminars. Some of the topics we cover are the care and handling of flowers and financial management techniques. We also conduct classes in the Pacific Rim teaching Western-style floral design."

Educators working with AFS are all experienced professionals in their various fields—from successful florists and floral designers to computer and financial experts.

Floral Designers

Commercial floral designers brighten almost every occasion, coordinating colors, shaping moods, creating atmosphere and beauty. They find work in commercial or specialty florist shops, as florist shop owners/designers, or as straight designers. A few find unusual and rewarding job settings such as consulting for the annual Rose Bowl Parade or commentating and judging at high level competitions or garden and flower shows.

They custom make arrangements to the specific needs of the client or fabricate their own creations using a few of the following popular design styles.

In a *pillowing* design, the arrangement resembles fleecy clouds. The flowers are placed up and down and are packed close together with some depth to them.

Pavé, meaning pavement, is the opposite of the pillowing design. With pavé design, everything is exactly the same size and very flat.

In a *parallel* design, the flowers are like soldiers standing at attention. The word *parallel* is from the Greek meaning side by side. The stems are straight up and down and parallel to each other. The arrangement can be vertical, horizontal, or diagonal.

New Convention has an architectural look. There are lines straight up and lines at a ninety-degree angle straight out. There are no forty-five-degree angles—in other words, nothing is leaning. This arrangement can resemble the skyline of a city seen on the horizon.

The *Romantic Look* is from the Victorian era, featuring little handheld posies, or Tussey Musseys, as they are called.

What It's Really Like

Al Mendoza, Floral Designer

In addition to owning Keepsake Flowers, Al Mendoza is also assistant director at the American Art Floral School. "I can take someone off the street and teach them design," Al says. "It's very mechanical. You establish your height, your width, your depth. The art part is where the talent comes in."

Training for Floral Designers

Many floral designers get their training working in a florist shop, learning as they go. They also attend seminars and workshops and take courses at floral design schools. The American Floral Art School, in business for more than fifty years, is one of the best known in the world. It offers an intensive three-week course, after which Al Mendoza says students will graduate as competent designers with a good understanding of the basics. "A three-week course," Al explains, "is enough to help a student get his or her foot in the door at a flower shop. But really, three weeks is not enough. The rest of the training comes from on-the-job experience. But it's a Catch-22 situation. It's difficult to get that first job without some sort of training. Our program helps to open the door."

There are no prerequisites to attend the school; no high school diploma or college degree is necessary to enter the field of floral design—although some academic preparation is recommended.

Al says, "I always tell any student who is coming to our school and planning on opening up a flower shop that it's great to know floral design, but it's more important to have a business degree than a floral degree. More businesses fail because they think of it as an art business rather than an actual commercial business. If people want to get their training through a college, they should major in business with a minor in floral design."

During the three-week program at the American Floral Art School, students study art and mechanics. "The art is what you see in a design, the mechanics are how you put it together," Al explains. "As a teacher, I stress more the mechanics than the art. The art will come to them naturally—the colors and the choice of flowers and the mixing—but the basic foundations of design are more important, what it is you need to make this whole composition come together. In the first week, we cover the seven principles of floral design: balance, accent, proportion, composition, unity, rhythm, and harmony and how they apply to funeral work. We gear the second week to using these principles and how they apply to everyday arrangements and party work. The third week we go into wedding work."

For further training, students attend seminars and workshops sponsored by local wholesalers or the AIFD, the American Institute of Floral Design, which is the professional association to which floral designers strive to belong. Admission to this organization is very competitive.

Earnings for Floral Designers

Although salaries vary in different parts of the country, entry-level floral designers with little or no experience can expect to earn minimum wage or a bit more. "In the flower business," Al Mendoza explains, "you're paid according to productivity and your design ability. Someone who is a good, fast, productive designer can make more money. It can go up to eight, nine, or ten dollars an hour. Then when you move into management positions, your salary goes up from there. Your pay scale is not based on how much schooling you've had or how much you know, but how much and how well you actually do."

Admission to the AIFD

Many floral designers, once they complete their training and have packed enough on-the-job experience under their belts, choose to apply for admission to the American Institute of Floral Designers. Membership in AIFD is very selective, and candidates must fulfill rigid qualifications and demonstrate advanced design ability.

The process of admission has two phases. In Phase I, candidates must submit a portfolio of their work, which includes photographs in seven specific categories: funeral design, hospital arrangement, dining table arrangement, holiday arrangement, bridal bouquet, their own specialties, and plans for a special wedding or party.

In Phase II, candidates must demonstrate their design ability on-site at various locations around the country determined by the AIFD. During a three-hour period, candidates complete designs in four categories: funeral arrangement, attendant's bouquet, arrangement for a business opening, and an interpretive design.

These floral design competitions add to a designer's prestige and upgrade the entire floriculture industry. Successful candidates earn the right to be distinguished by the letters "AIFD" after their name.

CHAPTER FIVE

Say It with Chocolate

F or some people, nothing elicits more passion and a sense of romance than wonderful, creamy, delicious, gourmet chocolate. Keep your diamonds and your perfume—just bring out the truffles!

Opening your own chocolate business or working for an established chocolatier will provide you with a steady taste of romance in your diet.

Let's see how one successful chocolatier got started and made his business work.

What It's Really Like

Richard Pearlman, Chocolatier

Richard Pearlman, president of Richard Pearlman Chocolates in Berkeley, California, started his gourmet chocolate business in 1995. He sells directly to customers through mail order and also sells wholesale to stores, caterers, and institutions.

The Romance of Chocolate

"If you think of chocolate as music, you can say that it's been at the top of the charts for four hundred years. In my experience, many women (and some men) are intensely passionate about chocolate. Nothing I ever worked on as a former PR person received nearly as strong a positive response as my chocolate business. I love it!

"My chocolate truffles have been served at many weddings, including my older stepdaughter's. I made a unique flavor for her—passion fruit and strawberry flavoring in a dark center coated with white chocolate.

"In some cases, brides have wanted me to supply the truffles, while the caterer supplied other things. The caterers tried them and have used me for other events.

"Chocolate and romance are made for each other. One man, a pilot in the marines, asked me to make truffles with wings for his girlfriend. So I had small white wings made from sugar gum paste and put them on each side of my Chocolate Passion (intense chocolate) truffles. Those went in a real red velvet heart-shaped box with French gold wire ribbon. She thought it was a wonderful gift."

Getting Started

"I was a self-employed PR consultant for sixteen years, including work in the gourmet food business. I've also taken intensive courses in French chocolate making, including one recently given by a talented French chef. It was a revelation in technique.

"I've always enjoyed chocolate. In 1982 I saw a recipe for chocolate truffles and started making them for friends and family. It's sort of the classic story. I did them at holidays and for special events.

"Several years ago people started asking me when I'd sell them. I said, honestly, when they were as good as anything around I'd sell them. When I felt they'd made it a few years ago, I went to work. At first it was just to local caterers and institutions (including UC Berkeley, my alma mater). Since then, I'm on my second commercial kitchen, have learned new skills, and have new products.

"As the business gets bigger. I'm planning to do as little paid advertising as possible. Before I do much, I'll use better customers as a focus group and find out where they go for information, then consider advertising in those areas. But direct mail is an approach that I will do more with this year, and I'm building a mailing list from various sources. Some are lists of businesses I know, and I may purchase targeted lists, too.

"I'm not planning on having shops for at least three years. The combination of overhead and other concerns make me feel that time and money are better spent developing wholesale, corporate, and direct mail sales.

"Having a shop or shops really depends on what you want to do with a business. I certainly wouldn't argue with anyone opening a shop for anything. But location is vital, especially with products like mine that really would need upscale sites. And upscale sites mean very high rents. So I'd rather put my resources elsewhere.

"On a personal level, I'd enjoy having a handful of shops at some point. But they have to be more than just an ego boost. And, since some investors will be involved in the future, it makes sense to point towards the more profitable approaches.

"I started things with less than $2,000 because my decision to go into the chocolate business came at the end of the 1991–95 recession, which had hurt my PR business. Because I'm about to have some investment and growth, discussing profits isn't realistic. A lot of expense will be required for growth. But the growth should result in profits. Down the road, I expect this to be a reasonably successful company with good profits for a small business."

All in a Day's Work

"My work is to create world-class chocolates. I only want to make chocolates that really thrill people, that they remember. Chocolates that excite people are what I'm all about. Chocolate is more than food—it's entertainment.

"Because this is a relatively new, growing business, no two days are the same. I spend at least as much time out of the kitchen as in it. I might spend a morning trying to track down a new supplier, see if the price of almonds is coming down, get out a few invoices, maybe pick up some supplies, or meet with a potential buyer. I enjoy the variety of my workday.

"Every day is busy one way or another. My theme is 'keep moving!' I'm always thinking about how things could be done better. Whether it's my chocolate truffles, packaging, the delivery process—everything is always being reexamined to make it better.

"Currently, I'm working in a commercial kitchen owned by a large bakery. I rent time when they're not using it. It's well equipped with stoves, convection ovens, walk-in refrigeration, freezers, and storage space. And it's very well maintained and clean, which is extremely important to me. It's also important to be in a place where I won't have the odors of onions, garlic, and so forth floating around while I work with melted chocolate.

"On a production day, I'll go over to the kitchen (currently available from noon to 2 A.M.), set up, and get to work. This may include chopping chocolate, roasting nuts, whipping up ganaches and fillings, molding some things, forming others. During a production day, I might make five hundred chocolate truffles or fifty pounds of almond-cranberry clusters or thirty pounds of filled chocolates.

"Between production, deliveries, paperwork, trying new things, working with suppliers, and so forth, even a slow week is probably at least fifty-five hours. Not a good idea to count! Currently, I am a one-man show, but soon I expect to have one or two full-time employees helping with chocolate production.

"But, in times of peak demand, I work as long as I can handle it. The month before Christmas, my shortest workday is usually sixteen hours. I joke that I am pioneering the 110-hour work week. Since most of that time is standing and working on production, I had some sore feet and legs!

"It helps that I was self-employed before starting the chocolate business. That way I was used to odd hours, fluctuating income, and the need to be resourceful. I've needed all the skills I've got and then some.

"You have to stay focused. I'm a talkative person with the exception being during chocolate production. You have to stay with things both mentally and physically. Otherwise, you can make a mistake and lose a batch of chocolate."

The Upsides

"One of the most gratifying things about making chocolates is seeing the response I get. I've had my chocolates literally demanded by one of the wealthiest people in the world, the Princess of Brunei. She'd had my truffles on one charter flight from the Bay Area. She and her retinue (about sixty people!) liked them so much that she demanded them on her next flight.

"A Parisian fashion designer said they were the only good chocolate she ever had in America. And, time after time, serious chocolate lovers have said that Richard Pearlman Chocolates are the best they've ever had. At my wife's workplace, I've been nicknamed 'The Truffle King.'

"The one comment I get, over and over, is that my customers never share their chocolates with anyone. And, three times now, women I didn't know told me my chocolates were better than sex! I don't blush easily, but I never got those responses about broccoli!

"I'm a person who likes (and needs) 'strokes' on a regular basis. So I admit that I love hearing these things.

"Beyond that, I see chocolate as an art form and deeply enjoy the ability to create things in my own way. I use outstanding ingredients and try to bring them together artfully. I want flavors and textures that are exciting and memorable. For instance, I used good Belgian chocolate for a while and then found better (and more expensive) French chocolate. There are some steps in my chocolate making that don't exist in recipe books—but they work! And at least a couple of products are unique (so far).

"Another gratifying part of this work is that so many great people have helped. The idea of a 'self-made' person is nonsense. Family, friends, neighbors, suppliers, people in the chocolate business have all offered both ideas and assistance. And they're excited about my business, too. My daughter has been a great help. One local chocolate maker generously offered the names of trusted suppliers. Another has helped with certain techniques. The support has been wonderful and reminds me that other people believe in my work, too.

"It's wonderful work, especially for a chocoholic like me. I love it, or I'd never work this hard. And it's nice to do something where people are always happy to see you!"

The Downsides

"It's not all chocolates and kudos. Money is a concern, as there are always attractive new things to buy, but the budget only stretches so far. We've definitely scaled back our lifestyle significantly, sticking to basic expenses and no frills, very few dinners out, and no real vacation in almost two years. For most people starting this kind of business, you have to sacrifice a lot, including your normal schedule, social schedule, and personal buying patterns.

"Production and delivery involves both physical labor and occasional fusses (such as big-city traffic snarls).

"Every once in a while, there may be a production mistake, so your work time is doubled. So far, staying focused, I've had relatively few mistakes. But a crucial piece of equipment might act up. Or a big customer may pay late."

Advice for Starting Your Own Chocolate Business

"If you want to start your own chocolate business, here are a few thoughts. Love making chocolates. Whatever you make, have quality throughout, including products, packaging, customer service, deliveries, etc.

"Have more money than you think you need. Just figure that whatever you expected to spend is probably half of what you need.

"Look to people around you for expertise. Suppliers, even other chocolate makers, can probably help you find things you need. Ask for their help but also plan to reciprocate. It's a two-way street.

"Take classes from good talent. It won't be cheap, but it's worth it.

"And, remember, you're not really in the food business. You're in the entertainment business. Put on a great show!"

For More Information

Richard Pearlman puts out a regular newsletter on his chocolate business. To be on his mailing list, contact him at

Richard Pearlman Chocolates
2550 Shattuck Avenue, #72
Berkeley, CA 94704

CHAPTER SIX

Say "I Do"

Have you ever attended a large wedding and wondered what went on behind the scenes to create such a well-coordinated event? Perhaps you already have a good idea. If so, you might see how a career as a wedding planner is ideally suited to your eye-to-detail romantic personality. Because it is careful attention to the details that makes events successful functions.

Planning the Big Event

Anyone who's been through it knows what's involved in pulling off a top-notch wedding. Just look at some of the details:

- Setting a date

- Obtaining the necessary licenses

- Arranging financing

- Reserving the location for the wedding ceremony

- Reserving the location for the reception

- Engaging the services of the person to perform the ceremony

- Choosing a menu

- Choosing or arranging for china and silverware

- For an outdoor event—ordering tables, cloths, tents, etc.

- Ordering flowers and coordinating their delivery

- Designing and printing napkins or matchbooks

- Hiring musicians

- Hiring a photographer

- Choosing bridesmaids, ushers, the best man, the flower girl, the ring bearer

- Ordering the cake and its centerpiece

- Creating an invitation list

- Designing and ordering invitations

- Addressing, stamping, and mailing invitations

- Arranging for transportation and/or accommodation for out-of-town guests

- Arranging for transportation to the ceremony and reception

There's more—the wedding dress, bridesmaid gowns, and clothing for the mother of the bride, the flower girl, and the groom. There are wedding accessories, too, such as the wedding album and the toast glasses. After all that, there's the honeymoon and all the travel plans that involves (see Chapter 10).

Often, with an event such as this not one person works alone to bring all the elements together. A bride, for example, would have the help of her mother or sisters or friends—or perhaps she'd use a bridal shop or hire a wedding consultant or planner.

Bridal Shop Owners and Wedding Coordinators

The vast majority of wedding planners are self-employed. Others work for hotels or bridal shops. Let's meet two successful wedding coordinators and see what they have to say.

What It's Really Like

Donna Lemire, Bridal Shop Owner

No day is more romantic—or more important—to a couple than their wedding day. And no one knows that better than Donna Lemire, owner of Illusions, a full-service bridal shop in Tyngsboro, Massachusetts. (Her website is listed in Appendix B.)

Donna Lemire opened her shop in 1994 and since then has been providing wedding apparel, accessories, and consultation and wedding coordination for a countless number of couples and their families.

She has worked in the field approximately twenty-four years, starting with wedding cakes and floral arrangements (see Chapter 4 for florist careers) and wedding consulting.

To train herself she has taken a variety of courses over the years, including cake decorating, floral design, and a wedding specialist course through Weddings Beautiful. (See later in this chapter and Appendix A for more information.)

That First Year

"Due to a personal tragedy in 1991 (I lost my son in an automobile accident), I needed to change careers. I was unhappy with my current life and wanted to work with happy people. I brought my cake business and florals, including some giftware, into the business first. Nice thought, but the people coming in were brides who needed more—for example, dresses.

"I knew it was time to either invest in inventory or give it up. My overhead was high, and I was virtually unknown. Even though my cakes and flowers were beautiful, they didn't pay the bills.

"I started by contacting bridal manufacturers and buying some dresses. Before I knew it, I had a fully stocked bridal shop. My first season I had twenty-four dresses, and now I have 140 bridal gowns (Moonlight, Demetrios, Private Label, Eden Bridal, Impressions Bridal, Loralie, Marabella, Sweetheart Bridal, Fink Boutique, Vow, Vogue, and Paula Varsalona), about 200 bridesmaid gowns, flower girl dresses, dresses for the mother of the bride, more than 150 headpieces, shoes, jewelry, and a full line of wedding accessories, such as unity candles, toast glasses, bridal garters, bridal gift sets, cake knives, and guest books. I also make silk floral arrangements and wedding cakes and have a range of rental items, including tuxedos, floral trees and arrangements, and card holders for the reception. I also have a decorated Victorian mailbox, a decorated bird cage, and a beautiful gazebo.

"In addition, I consult and sell wedding invitations, and, as a coordinator, I have the contacts to arrange a full wedding, regardless of budget.

"But my first year was difficult because I was virtually unknown. I took out ads in all local newspapers in the bridal section. I also got advertising in the bridal magazines—which worked the best. It is also important to advertise in the Yellow Pages of the telephone book. An 800 number adds credibility. I did church bulletins, place mats (didn't work.) I did a few bridal fashion shows. The most important thing is to get your name out there. I also joined the Better Business Bureau, but that was also a waste of money. You don't need to be a member; just do a good job. If there are no complaints against you, no one can hurt you—or help you.

"Most of my new business that first year came from referrals. I received numerous thank you notes and pictures of previous brides and grooms."

Wedding Coordinator

"Being a coordinator enables me to take my services one step further. A couple can walk into my shop with no direction and walk out having everything they need with a minimum of leg work. Even if they do not require a coordinator, I supply them with business cards for whatever they need. There is, of course, no charge for a referral. I tell them to meet with the people, ask for references, view their work, and not commit to anything until they have met with a few vendors for each service required.

"Of course, if they hire me for the coordinating, I interview and hire the vendors. Being a full-service shop requires me to put more time into my clients. I am concerned with the wedding, not just what my clients choose to wear."

Location, Location, Location

"My location is bad for walk-in business but great because I am easy to find. I am right off a major highway. Walk-in business is very important for visibility the first year, but the rent is high for most malls with high traffic. It's a catch-22. I made sure I kept enough surplus money available to pay the rent for a year."

Wedding Romance

"The romance of the business comes from two different aspects of the business. Usually when the bride puts on a dress that she knows she wants, I can tell by the tears in her eyes and usually her mother's. The second moment is when I am coordinating the wedding and the groom cries when he sees his bride approaching. Those are my two favorite moments. I do get more personal satisfaction doing the coordinating because I interact more with the bride and groom. When the limo drives up, I am the one who takes the bride out of the car. I always get the last minute hug, which always warms my heart. I usually get one from the groom when I pin the boutonniere on him as well. Just knowing that you were instrumental in participating in the most important day of a couple's life gives you a natural high. Getting there sometimes is a challenge, as I have said earlier, but, somehow, it always seems worth it in the end. The only people who survive this business are the ones who genuinely love it. It has brought me closer to my own husband being around so much happiness. Most of the time, I would have to classify it as a labor of love. I spent two hours last night with a bride not sure of her feelings. We talked until long after I closed the shop. Sometimes when family gets too involved in the festivities, these brides need someone to talk to who isn't Mom or Dad. They are looking for someone to tell them the prenuptial jitters are common. They are so afraid to tell their parents they have doubts because of the money being spent, they keep it all inside until some of them are so miserable they don't enjoy the time before their wedding. How many times have we heard a bride say, 'I'll be glad when this is over.'

"By having a wedding coordinator to listen and talk with, my brides are not so likely to get overwhelmed with the mounting questions they are afraid to ask a relative. Along with the festivities goes anxiety, fear, and being able to accept change gracefully. It is against our nature as human beings to cope with one of those feelings at a time, let alone all of them at once. It is enough for any bride to ask herself if she is doing the right thing. When I am asked about any of these things, my first question is always, 'Do you love him?' If the answer is yes, then I proceed with the stories of the many other brides that I have had the same conversations with.

"I guess the real romance is with my brides and their innermost feelings. I try to be at the church, even if I have not been hired to coordinate the wedding. It is a service-oriented business, and the commitment is enormous, if you are doing your job the way you should be. It is the most important dress this woman is ever going to buy, and she must feel absolutely beautiful in it. Without that, any shop owner is doing her a disservice. I never try to make the sale until I have made the bride happy. Anything less than that is not only stealing her money but stealing her moment. Choosing a wedding dress is an emotional moment, and it has to be treated with respect."

A Seasonal Business

"How business is depends on the season. In the Northeast, bridal season starts in April and continues strong through the end of June. It picks up again in September and runs through the second week of November. I am extremely busy sometimes with several weddings in one weekend.

"I get all the dresses and tuxedos ready for pickup, and I get all the things delivered that need to be delivered with the help of my husband, my best friend. No matter what has to be done, he's there and waiting for my schedule, which is sometimes very demanding."

The Upsides and Downsides

"The part of my job I love the most is pleasing a bride. Not an easy accomplishment. Remember, these women are overindulged from the moment they become engaged. Mom and Dad spoil them because they know they are getting ready to let go, and the emotions are running high. However, they forget that you may be working with thirty to thirty-five brides at a time. It takes a lot of patience and hand holding. If it is appreciated, you don't mind so much.

"A lot of these women are very sweet until a few weeks before their wedding. Then, they all turn into Sybil. I am sure I could write a book at this point in my career, some of it good, some of it leaving me with the question if I made the right choice. I guess that is a question we all ask ourselves from time to time.

"The bottom line is that it takes a lot of money to operate this kind of business. The inventory costs are high. Unfortunately, you can't sell off the rack unless you buy discontinued dresses. Discontinued dresses are a short-term answer to a long-term commitment to your manufacturers. If you have a dress that a bride falls in love with, and it's two sizes to small, you can't order a discontinued dress. You have to keep a dress in stock for a minimum of two seasons while it is still currently selling. After a couple of seasons of sweat and being stepped on, you are lucky to break even on your cost.

"The answer for success is volume. It takes a long time to establish a solid reputation. Most businesses see a profit after three years. I would say that if you make a profit after five in the bridal business, you have made it."

Charging for Your Services

"Most consultants charge for their services in two ways. Some get a percentage of the entire wedding. Initially the charge on a percentage basis is 10 percent. As you become more successful, you may charge 15 percent.

"Others such as myself charge a flat fee of anywhere from $25 to $50 per hour—it depends on how little or how much you do. I have other income from my shop, dresses, tuxedo rentals, and other accessories. If I were working from my home, as some coordinators do, obviously I would be a little more flexible with my fee schedule. I have a business within a business, so I am obligated to other duties within my shop. Most of the coordinating I do is based on an hourly basis. I feel that is fair to my bride.

"If I ever sell the shop and decide to strictly do wedding coordinating, I will probably charge a percentage of the wedding. I have to believe it is the most lucrative because most weddings exceed $10,000. At 10 percent, a coordinator can expect a salary of $1,000.

"With the income from my dresses and other things, I usually make anywhere around that per wedding, after expenses. I guess it all works out. The shop is a double-edged sword; the expenses are high, but the brides come to me. I am sure I could book any number I want, but I prefer to screen them first before I decide if I want to coordinate the wedding. Sometimes it is like opening Pandora's box. Some I would prefer to stay away from."

Advice for Potential Bridal Shop Owners

"My advice to anyone venturing on this endeavor would be to seek out a partner with the same commitment. It is too much for one person to handle alone. With the kind of initial investment needed for a successful shop, it would be nice to share the expense. Hiring someone to help out is a nice thought, but it takes hours, sometimes days to sell one of these dresses. Most people do not have enough patience unless an investment is on the line.

"It takes a serious commitment and a lot of money. This should not be minimized. Only a person with unlimited resources should make this venture alone. I can't stress this enough. Unfortunately, by the time the shop reaches a successful status, you could have spent at least $100,000 in stock.

"In addition, research bridal manufacturers carefully and thoroughly. Stay away from designers with high minimums or that make you pay for advertising. Do not pay large amounts of money to open accounts. Don't always rely on information in bridal magazines to help make decisions regarding what you want to carry. A perfect example is one company in particular that advertises heavily in bridal magazines. Bridal shops pay in excess of $1,000 per season for the privilege of selling its dresses. The company requires a $4,000 opening order and buries you season after season with minimums. Any new bridal shop trying to start a successful business would be doomed almost from the start. The quality is questionable at best, and you would have to sell tons of them to begin to make a profit. It is not worth the investment, nor is it worth carrying the line. Before a shop knows it, they have to get rid of some better-selling lines just to support that one.

"You have to genuinely love the business to operate an honest bridal shop. It takes twelve to fourteen hours a day, six days a week. Most weeks on the seventh day, there's the paperwork.

"Decorating a shop is also very important. You must spend money on flowers and lattice. Soft colors and a comfortable seating area are essential. I have a television with a VCR to show videos of weddings I have done or ideas that I might want to share with a bride. It is a very visual business, and if you plan on selling $1,000 dresses, you better look like you mean it.

"Presentation is extremely important in this business. You have to make them want to stay in your shop forever. They have to feel comfortable. If they think the shop is dirty, or the people are rude or the dresses are dirty, there is another shop right down the street."

Training to Be a Wedding Consultant

One way to prepare yourself for a wedding consultant role would be to take a specialized home-study training program. Weddings Beautiful offers such a service, as well as continuing-education seminars and courses.

After the course, you earn a Wedding Beautiful Certified Wedding Specialist certificate. Through the course, you will study every facet of a wedding and learn the preferred way as well as alternatives. According to Weddings Beautiful:

A Certified Wedding Specialist can save the bride time and money. She is trained in etiquette, procedure, coordinating and directing weddings and planning receptions. She knows the role of divorced parents, who pays for what, whose name(s) appear on the invitation, what style wedding gowns look best on different figure types, who dances with whom and in what order, how to set tables properly, the difference in china, porcelain and pottery and how to deal with misunderstandings between brides and their parents or brides and grooms. She provides a worry-free wedding for the wedding party because she knows the rules and when to break them.

While she gives proper advice, she will not impose her own ideas. She will guide, listen, plan, organize and be a friend. Because she is professionally and objectively involved, she will

*be the diplomat when controversy arises, coordinating details
and managing issues.*

Both established wedding coordinators and those who are
interested in starting a business coordinating weddings can benefit from the training. In addition, Weddings Beautiful courses
cater to those in wedding-related businesses—florists, photographers, caterers, gift registries, jewelers, bridal shop owners, and
others. Courses are self-study, and you proceed at your own pace.
Most people take six to twelve months for completion. Contact
Weddings Beautiful for more information. The address is provided in Appendix A.

Mary Tribble, Event Planner

Mary Tribble is the president and owner of Mary Tribble Creations, an event planning and production company located in
Charlotte, North Carolina. In 1982 she earned her B.A. in art
history from Wake Forest University in Winston-Salem, North
Carolina. She is also one of forty people in the country to have
earned the Certified Special Event Professional (CSEP) designation from the International Special Event Society (ISES). She
has also attended countless continuing education courses
through industry conventions. And she is also asked frequently
to speak on event planning at regional and national conventions.

How Mary Tribble Got Started

"I was working at an advertising agency as an account executive
when one of my clients asked the agency to plan a grand opening event for the new offices. As a special project, it ended up
being my responsibility. It was a huge event—a black tie gala
with a laser light show—and I loved every minute of the planning. I knew I wanted to be involved in events from that time on.
At first, we opened a small division at the agency for event

planning, but I soon went out on my own. I was twenty-four at the time.

"I started with nothing more than a Rolodex, sitting on my bed in my apartment. No computer, nothing. I got a loan from a friendly investor for $5,000, which tided me over until the checks started coming in. That was eleven years ago.

"After about two years in business, I rented a small office, then hired my first person, who is still with me. I now have three employees—which is a gracious plenty as far as I'm concerned.

"Now that the industry has gotten so much more sophisticated, I'm not sure I'd be able to get by the way I did back then. Clients want event planners who are educated in the industry, carry all the proper insurance—and all that takes money. I have very nice offices in downtown Charlotte, and I think that adds credibility to my company.

"Now, because I've been around so long, I get a lot of my business through word of mouth—but I still have to market my services. That's usually through phone calls and sending out my brochure to prospects.

"I don't do much advertising—not even in the Yellow Pages. But, I'm very active in the chamber of commerce and am a member of our convention and visitors bureau and the International Special Events Society. A lot of business comes through networking with those groups."

A Typical Day

"It's crazy, stress-filled, but fun. The other day would be a good example of a typical day:

- 7:30 A.M.—Meeting with a client about a huge event we're planning for the millennium.

- 9:00 A.M.—Back to the office. Reworked a budget for a wedding client we have. (The mother wanted it *all*, but the father had called me into his office—without his wife—to tell me what he was willing to spend.)

- 10:30 A.M.—Meeting with a client about another event.
- noon—Off to exercise, then lunch at desk.
- 1:00 P.M.—Sales calls during the first part of the afternoon.
- 2:30 P.M.—Brainstorming meeting with staff. Interrupted by call from a client to put together an event in a week. Reconvened staff to brainstorm again.
- 4:00 P.M.—Worked on writing up a proposal.
- 5:30 P.M.—Visited a potential rehearsal dinner site.
- 6:30 P.M.—Home.

"My days are rarely, if ever, relaxed. A typical day has three to six meetings, plus phone calls, deadlines for proposals, budgeting, worrying about payroll, dealing with employees' problems, making sales calls, doing diagrams of event layouts, trudging around construction sites, meeting with vendors and clients, fielding phone calls from people who want to pick my brain about the event biz, and so forth.

"The work atmosphere is usually what I'd described as 'frantic fun.' I try to run a flexible company with a sense of humor—practical jokes are encouraged—but I expect everyone to roll up their sleeves and get the job done.

"In the busy season, I work sixty to sixty-five hours a week. When it's less busy, about fifty. My employees work about forty-five to fifty hours, since they only work events they are assigned. (I'm usually at them all.)

Wedding Bell Blues

"Weddings can be especially difficult to plan, because there are so many personalities involved. With a corporate client, I'm usually answering to one person, and that person has usually reached a consensus with his or her staff as to what the event should be. With a wedding, the bride, the MOB (Mother of the

Bride), the FOB (Father of the Bride), the in-laws, and the groom all have different expectations.

"The bride—and the MOB—have been dreaming of this day for twenty-some years, so their expectations are very high. The FOB is usually worried about what the costs will be and can't understand why the MOB wants to spend $2,000 on place card holders. There have been times when the MOB, bride, and FOB are diametrically opposed, and I've had to step into some very tense situations, acting as mediator. It can be a very emotional experience for all concerned, and it's my job to stay calm and bring everyone to a consensus.

"It's also my job to exceed the twenty-some years of expectations—create a fairy-tale wedding that the bride will remember forever—whatever her style or taste. One month that might mean a casual lakeside wedding with a rustic wedding canopy covered with lavender, roses, and vines. The next it could be a glittering gold wedding patterned after Versailles in a hotel ballroom, with huge gold candelabra centerpieces.

"That particular glittering gold wedding was something I had only three and half weeks to plan—and it was for five hundred people! The groom's mother was ill, and the wedding had been set for six months off. But all were concerned that she might not make it. So, BAM! We had to plan a huge gala in less than a month—in a different hotel than had been originally reserved.

"For all the events I work with, we come up with the ideas, then plan the whole thing from start to finish—invitations, catering, decorating, special effects, entertainment, etc. We contract all of that out, though. We don't keep lasers in stock!

"Paying attention to the details is the most important part of event planning. We can come up with all the wonderful themes in the world, but if we don't interpret them with details, they mean nothing. When we plan an event, everything—invitations, decorations, entertainment, place cards, gifts, signage—is selected to enhance the concept of the event.

"Also, the day-to-day planning is very detail oriented. We have to imagine an event from the time someone gets the invitation to how they will get there, where they will park, who will greet them, how the event will begin, and how it will end.

"For every event, we create a schedule for setup, which is an hour-by-hour outline of everything that will happen leading up to the event. Sometimes, if it's a complicated event, that document can be ten to twelve pages long. We also create a show schedule that outlines the event itself."

The Romance Makes It All Worthwhile

"The 'romance' of my job usually comes when the bride walks into the reception for the first time and sees the effect we have created. If she gasps, I know we've done our job.

"What I like most about my work is the satisfaction that I've surpassed the client's dreams and expectations. The gasp factor. Also, I like the diversity—no day is ever the same, and I do get to spend a good deal of my time with creative people, brainstorming new ideas and coming up with new challenges.

"I also get a rush from the stress the events create. I like to problem solve on my toes and come up with quick and innovative solutions."

The Downside

"The long hours are a downside, though. It's not too uncommon for us to work eighteen to twenty hours with no break—and I'm getting too old for that! I work a lot of weekends and evenings. Other downsides are dealing with all the details of the event, which is why I have employees. I like to conceptualize the event, but the drudgery of all the phone calls and meetings on minute things can be tiresome."

The Finances Involved

"Different planners charge different ways, and it's up to you to figure out what works best in your market. A way to do this would be, first of all, to join an association for event or wedding planning so you can network with others in your area. The Association of Bridal Consultants is strictly for wedding planners. The International Special Events Society covers the whole industry. (See Appendix A for addresses.)

"Having said that, some people charge an hourly fee, some charge a percentage of the overall budget, and others charge a combination of both. Usually, total fees will equal roughly 15 to 30 percent of the overall budget, using whichever method you choose.

"I personally always charge some kind of planning fee, even if I'm adding a percentage, because I think it's important for the client to perceive value in your services.

"In terms of potential annual earnings, that can vary widely from market to market, as you can imagine. I'd say for the first year or so not to count on earning much higher than in the twenties—you've got to develop a reputation first and then get business by recommendations from satisfied clients.

"Because most weddings are planned at least eight months out, it will be some time before those contracts come in. After three or four years of exemplary service to your clients, you could expect $40,000 or so, depending on the city you serve. This could go much higher in large metropolitan areas, but a planner in a smaller market may never exceed that level.

"Word of warning when considering wedding planning as a career: don't forget that weddings happen on weekends! You need to be prepared for a very heavy work load during the wedding season."

Advice from Mary Tribble

"Education, education, education! Just because you planned your sorority rush parties doesn't mean you can plan events professionally. We take on a great deal of responsibility when we put a thousand people in a hotel ballroom.

"Is the event safe? Does our layout meet fire codes? Are our linens, draping, candles approved by the fire department? Is the event handicapped accessible? Does the caterer meet health code requirements? Do we have enough liability insurance?

"You have to think about worker's comp and if we have permission to record and/or play licensed music. Are we following union regulations? Will the electricity carry the load of the equipment we've brought in?

"Planning events is not all fun and games, and you must make sure you're providing your client with a safe and secure event. You need to stay atop of the cutting-edge trends and make sure your clients are getting the best services possible.

"The International Special Events Society has chapters all over the world, most of which offer monthly educational meetings. George Washington University now offers a degree in events management. *Special Events Magazine* hosts an annual convention for three thousand event producers, with great education sessions. There are plenty of avenues now for you to get the education that even I didn't have when I started out.

"Even if you don't go for a specific event planning degree, degrees in public relations, marketing, or hotel/hospitality management can prepare you to some extent. Public relations courses very often include sections on events.

"In addition to education, you need hands-on experience. Volunteer on a committee for a local nonprofit organization's fundraiser. Intern at an event production company, hotel, or catering firm. The experience you receive will be a great investment."

Do You Have What It Takes?

"The perfect event planner personality? You need to be a left brain/right brain person—you need the creative side to come up with new and exciting ideas, but you also need the detail side to execute them. That's a tough combination.

"You also need to thrive on stress and learn not to panic in bad situations. You need to be quick on your toes, and you need to be a negotiator, and you need to have a calming influence on people. Our clients need someone calm and relaxed in the face of the controlled chaos."

Becoming Certified as an Event Planner

Contact the International Special Events Society for information on its certification procedures. (The address is in Appendix A.) The group will send a form outlining the "point system," which determines whether or not you can sit for the exam. You accumulate points based on the number of years you have spent in the business, attending continuing education classes, and other criteria. Once you have earned enough points, you sit for a written exam.

The process is not necessarily an easy one, but it pays off two ways: respect from your peers and raised standing in the event community, and you can use it as a marketing tool for clients, who will usually be fairly impressed when you tell them what the CSEP designation means.

CHAPTER SEVEN

Cater the Affair

Wedding Caterers

C aterers share an important role in making any wedding a success. Although years afterward guests will most likely remember the blushing bride and not what was served for dinner, a bad meal presented unprofessionally will make an unpleasant, lasting experience for everyone.

Caterers come to their profession through many avenues. Some earn degrees in hotel and restaurant management; others learn on the job working their way up before going out on their own. Here are two caterers who are both romantics at heart.

What It's Really Like

Sherry Ebertshauser, Caterer

Sherry Ebertshauser owns a small catering company that she operates from a home office in Louisville, Kentucky.

"The task of catering is to be very organized. Most would think this is done by going here and there, just gathering food. But truly, paperwork is your number one helper. To make sure you know your clients, even their favorite colors, it is important to take notes. Then you go here and there and make sure you cover every factor—even things that would not come under catering.

"For example, good caterers know that they may find themselves setting the timetable or schedule so the events flow smoothly. At a wedding, the mother of the bride wants to be able to enjoy herself, too, so you can help by seeing to her guests.

"Another example is knowing which photo shots are most important and directing the person in charge to see to it or making sure the men are where they are supposed to be. Men do not do well at weddings.

"A typical day for me begins at 4:40 in the morning, setting goals that I must meet by the end of the day. Early to rise is the way it is in the catering business.

"The real drawback is the hours, but I would never suggest that is a negative unless you are starting a family."

The Romance in Catering

"We all love romance, and many people will go out of their way to see that a loved one is given a special surprise. A young man gives you, the caterer, a ring and asks you to hide it in the bread you're about to serve. Or he asks the manager to have the server drop it into her wine glass.

"To my knowledge no one has broken a tooth or choked this way. The trouble comes from trying to get the bride to be, who is not a bread eater, to take the slice of bread. The poor man did all but shove the bread down her throat.

"As I watched, he kept offering her the bread basket, and she kept saying 'no.' He was so flustered that I walked over to the table and asked if she had ever tried our honey butter, upon which she finally did take the bread—and then saw the ring.

"It wasn't as romantic as the man wanted the occasion to be, with a manager standing over him while she teared up and began to cry. As he asked the magic question, I slowly backed away.

"With dropping a ring in a wine glass, I have to stand by to make sure the bride to be doesn't swallow it. One man insisted on her favorite red wine, but I said no way. It had to be white so she could see the ring and not swallow it accidentally. It always works out well, though."

The Thrill in Catering

"Unless you actually know the thrill of serving the public it would be hard for anyone to understand. The thrill . . . yes, there are many forms. If you serve the public in fast food, there is nothing more exciting than to see how fast you can get that order prepared. If you work in the area of fine dining, or 'white linen,' as I like to call it, the thrill comes into play from watching your customers closely and seeing that their every need is met, the food is excellent, the wine perfect, and the service exceptional. There is no second guessing here. A good manager, as well as a server, knows how to read the signs, and when the job is done that thrill is there. It comes from not only monetary gain but from the satisfaction of knowing you have added memories of a pleasant evening into a person's life.

"When you cater, there is a thrill also. You get to know your clients on a first-name basis. You become a part of the affair—most of my clients even send an invitation to me. If you do your job well, you can become a part of their family and will make friends for life. This year I found myself still catering, even though I have retired. People who are renewing their vows, for example, and want the same meal I prepared for them years ago. Now, that's a thrill!"

How Sherry Ebertshauser Got Started

"I started working for Pet Foods. They purchased the chain of Stuckey's stores, which began my training in the fast food industry and management.

"After spending some time with the company, I put together plans for my own business and in 1978 purchased a restaurant called the Scallion. The Scallion was a small restaurant, open daily, serving homemade soups and sandwiches that I prepared myself. Thus my cooking experience and catering began, doing weddings and box lunches, etc.

"The Scallion is now closed. Rather than sell it and take the chance my reputation might suffer, I closed it down and now work out of my home. Most of my work today comes from the years I did catering from the restaurant on the side. I do weddings and small parties, preparing the food myself."

Advice from Sherry Ebertshauser

"Take as many jobs as you can from various food chains. Their training is valuable. Work in all areas—know what a dishwasher's work is like, for example.

"If I were to start again, I would also take classes in becoming a chef. Although I am a caterer and I do give cooking classes and prepare most of my own food, I am a basically a manager.

"And always remember, a catered event such as a wedding is a memory in the happening. People have planned and worked most of their lives for this day. When it finally arrives, they are worn out and are living a dream, as if it is not actually happening. So, you must be the one to make sure that dream is concrete.

"Today, with video cameras, a caterer's work is even harder, staying one step ahead, not reacting to a mishap, but planning ahead so the mishap will not occur. No one, especially the bride, wants a taped reminder of a blunder."

Frances Haberkost, Caterer

Frances Haberkost is the retired owner of Fran's Catering in Akron, Ohio. She worked as a caterer for almost forty years.

How Frances Haberkost Got Started

"I had extensive experience in food preparation from having worked in restaurants since I was sixteen years old. I went to

Hammel Actual Business College for two years, taking secretarial and business courses, which were later very applicable to another position I held at Akron City Hospital. But the good business sense applied to catering, too, because I did all the bookkeeping, billing, and any other paperwork connected with my catering business.

"I first started catering around forty years or so ago, when a friend of mine asked me to do her daughter's wedding. It was a simple but elegant affair—just finger sandwiches, cake, punch, mints, and nuts. We decorated my friend's basement and had about 125 people there. Even a basement can be 'transformed' with a little creativity, some ideas I had (based on magazines and pictures I'd seen), and a little imagination!

"I always enjoyed putting the event together, like the pieces of a puzzle. New ideas were always popping into my head, and I felt such a sense of satisfaction when I could create something beautiful from scraps and materials lying about the house. My basement was my 'workshop.' When my children were small and needed me at home, I converted part of the basement into a gift shop. This required me to have a vendor's license, both for tax purposes and so I could purchase supplies wholesale. I used this same license when I began catering, as no other permit was required at that time."

What It Takes

"It takes real dedication to be a successful caterer, and you have to be willing to work very long hours, because you just can't stop until the entire job's completed. Cooking was always one of my favorite things to do, and making each recipe from scratch not only made the food taste better, it was fun! I always insisted on the best cuts of meat, the choicest ingredients for homemade salads, relish trays, and breads, because I wouldn't want to serve something to other people that I wouldn't want myself.

"Everyone in the family was involved in the business with their own jobs to do, and everyone would work together to do some of the tasks, such as loading and unloading the cars. Sometimes the weddings were so big I'd have to hire other friends of mine to help, but everyone would look very professional in front of the guests. I bought white uniforms for each of us, which we wore along with a white apron. Everyone's hair had to be up off the face or in a hair net if it was long, so as not to get into the food. We even had uniform shoes. Our appearance was very 'professional.'

"We never had our own hall—which had always been a dream of mine. In fact, it's something I'd insist on today! We stored all the equipment and supplies in our basement, so for each reception we'd have to box everything, bring it upstairs and load it into one of our two cars, drive to the rented reception hall, unload everything, and set up. Then, when the reception was over, everything had to be repacked, loaded into cars (again), and driven home. Then, even though by now everyone was exhausted, everything had to be carried back inside the house. Often we would start the cleanup the next day. We always used either china, glass, or plastic dishes (never paper), so there were plenty of dishes to wash!

"In the basement we had two large stationary washtubs, which came in very handy. We also used silverware, and the punch cups were glass or plastic, so we had those to wash as well. I loved using silver, and we eventually owned quite a lot of pieces, from a complete service, including a coffeepot, teapot, sugar, creamer and tray, a tea service, to silver water pitchers and candelabras. They all required special care and cleaning, but how elegant they looked when glistening on the table, ready for service!

"In hindsight, it seems as if it was an awful lot of extra work, but anyone can throw a party together using paper. I wanted to provide something extra special, something the bride would cherish for the rest of her life. Attention to detail was the key. Everything was carefully orchestrated, from the dressmaker's pearl-topped pins to hold the fabric skirts on the table to the wedding cake itself, with its individually designed cake top.

"Each bride was unique, and so was her cake top. One of my favorites was a handmade Styrofoam spiral staircase, with little dolls dressed in fabric that I matched to the bridesmaids' dresses. "I started renting a punch fountain about five years into catering. It was more dramatic than a cut-glass punch bowl. It was quite an attraction, as it was one of the first things a guest would see upon entering the reception hall. I'd set it up on its own round table, covered with a white linen tablecloth and skirt of one of the wedding colors, which was then covered with white netting. The fountain itself was silver with ornate fonts all around it, and it looked quite charming and mystical with dry ice vapor misting the punch as it trickled down into the bowl.

"Before we started renting the fountain, we used cut-glass punch bowls. I still recall with fondness how for Christmas one year, my husband (knowing how much I love shiny and pretty things) gave me another cut-glass punch bowl with one hundred matching cups.

The Romance of the Job

"Each detail you attend to will add to the 'air of romance' and make this an extra-special event. Some very popular ideas were the guest book, which stood separately beside the cloth-covered gift table, with its feather quill pen ready for the guests to arrive. The tables would all have a satin ribbon streamer down the cloth-covered center in a color to match the bridesmaids' dresses.

"I always decorated the tables where the guests would sit with something special, too. Down the center of each white tablecloth would run a satin ribbon to match one of the wedding colors. In the middle of each table I'd place a decoration. Sometimes it would be a brandy snifter half filled with colored water, with a floating candle inside. Once it was a bride doll with a daisy face (the bride especially loved daisies).

"I enjoyed varying these—it gets boring if you do the same thing every time. Here's where you can use some of your creativity.

"The food tables were all elegantly decorated with linen table-cloths and fabric skirts that matched the wedding colors. The center table would be round. Reserved for the cake, it would always be a special attraction. Satin ribbon roses would often be spaced every foot or so along the tail edge. Surrounding the cake would be engraved napkins, silver forks, and little silver bowls of mints and nuts. Silver coffee and tea sets would grace a nearby table. Attention to detail is very important. I wanted the reception to be as special as the bride herself. This would be a day she'd never forget."

The Upsides and Downsides

"The creativity involved and the chance to 'make the event something really special' are the definite pluses here! This is your chance to 'be your own boss.' It's definitely both a challenging and rewarding career. You can literally make something from nothing.

"I least liked cleaning the hall up beforehand. Not having my own hall was a major setback. We'd go to various rented halls to set up our equipment and find a huge mess left from the people who were there before us."

Calculating Your Fees

"I offered each client a choice of three different menus, each with a set price per person. I would calculate this price based on the price per pound of the meat at the time (this fluctuated the most), the cost of all the other food, labor, and a reasonable percentage markup for profit.

"I suggest that a person just starting out add no more than 20 percent. You don't want to overprice yourself, or the client will choose someone else! Of course, back then I didn't have to worry about worker's compensation and insurance costs as you would today.

"For more help in setting prices, beginners should do research and find out what other people are charging for comparable services. The more people you contact, the better understanding you'll have of the competition. Your potential earning power is only limited by your imagination and how hard you want to work!"

Advice for Getting Started

"Don't start unless you're really determined to be a success. Also, have a clause in your contract that the people who hire you will pay to replace anything broken or stolen. And people will steal.

"Check with your local chamber of commerce and the 'One-Stop Business Center' for a current list of licensing requirements. Have your own facility if at all possible. There's always a shortage of halls, and with your own facility you have better control. Lastly, don't be cheap. Anybody can use paper supplies and decorate with crepe paper, but quality speaks for itself."

CHAPTER EIGHT

Finishing Touches

The table is set, the food is ready, the gown is hanging safely in its garment bag, waiting to be donned. All that's left to do is the finishing touches—to help the bride and the wedding party shine on her special day.

If you enjoy the romance of engagement parties and weddings and other special occasions, and you also have a knack for the "beauty business," cosmetology might be the right career for you.

While many cosmetologists work for beauty salons, there are many who freelance—working in people's homes or at department stores, taking care of individual clients.

Cosmetology encompasses the following job titles:

- hair stylists, who shampoo, cut, and style hair

- makeup artists, who advise on and apply makeup

- manicurists, who clean, shape, and polish customer's fingernails and toenails

- electrologists, who remove hair from skin by electrolysis

- estheticians, who cleanse and beautify the skin

Some cosmetologists specialize in just one of the above areas; others gain training in several.

Training for Cosmetologists

Although all states require cosmetologists to be licensed, the qualifications necessary to obtain a license vary. Generally, a person must have graduated from a state-licensed cosmetology school, pass a physical examination, and be at least sixteen years old.

In addition, education requirements vary from state to state—some require graduation from high school, while others require as little as an eighth-grade education. In a few states, completion of an apprenticeship can substitute for graduation from a school, but very few cosmetologists learn their skills in this way. Applicants for a license usually are required to pass a written test and demonstrate an ability to perform basic cosmetology services.

Some states have reciprocity agreements that allow licensed cosmetologists to practice in a different state without additional formal training. Other states do not recognize training or licenses obtained in another state; consequently, people who wish to become cosmetologists should review the laws of the state in which they want to work before entering a training program.

Public and private vocational schools offer daytime or evening classes in cosmetology. These programs usually last six to twelve months. An apprenticeship program can last from one to two years.

Formal training programs include classroom study, demonstrations, and practical work. Students study the basic services—haircutting, facial massaging, and hair and scalp treatments—and, under supervision, practice on customers in school clinics. Most schools also teach unisex hairstyling and chemical styling. Students attend lectures covering the use and care of instruments, sanitation and hygiene, and recognition of certain skin ailments.

Instruction also is given in selling and general business practices. There are also advanced courses for experienced hair stylists in coloring and the sale and service of hairpieces. Most schools teach hairstyling of men's as well as women's hair.

After graduating from a training program, students can take the state licensing examination. The examination consists of a written test and, in some cases, a practical test of cosmetology skills. A few states include an oral examination in which the applicant is asked to explain the procedures he or she is following while taking the practical test. In some states, a separate examination is given for people who want only a manicurist license or a facial care license.

Many schools help their graduates find jobs. During their first months on the job, new workers are given relatively simple tasks, such as giving shampoos, or are assigned to perform the simpler hairstyling patterns. Once they have demonstrated their skills, they are gradually permitted to perform the more complicated tasks, such as coloring hair or applying a permanent.

Job Outlook

Overall employment of cosmetologists is expected to grow faster than the average for all occupations through the year 2005. Population growth, rising incomes, and a growing demand for the services that they provide will stimulate the demand for these workers. Within this occupation, however, different employment trends are expected.

Cosmetologists will account for virtually all of the employment growth, reflecting the continuing shifts in consumer preferences to more personalized services and in salons to full-service, unisex establishments. Demand for manicurists and for cosmetologists who are trained in nail care will be particularly strong.

Earnings

Cosmetologists receive income either from commissions and tips or wages and tips. Most full-time cosmetologists earn somewhere between $20,000 and $30,000, including tips. Earnings depend on the size and location of the shop, the number of hours worked, customers' tipping habits, competition from other salons, and the cosmetologist's ability to attract and hold regular customers.

Those who freelance set their own fees and work as many hours as they choose. Although freelancers often choose self-employment because of the convenient hours, those carrying a full-time freelance load can earn much more than a cosmetologist employed by a salon or department store.

The following two cosmetologists will give you an idea of what the field is like.

What It's Really Like

Mary Kern, Freelance Makeup Artist

Mary Kern is a freelance makeup artist working as an independent contractor in Wall, New Jersey. She does makeup for special occasions, traveling to an individual's home, as well as freelance work for cosmetic companies in department store chains.

Training = Selling

"Most cosmetic companies do have training sessions. Unfortunately, most of it will consist of selling techniques. The primary goal of most companies is to sell, sell, sell, and it will get drilled into your head until you want to scream. The bottom line is if you get a job for a company with a treatment line, they want you to sell treatment products (because they will produce higher volume sales). This is a downfall to the job if your main interest is doing makeup."

Some Pointers for You

"If your interest is in being a makeup artist, here are a couple of pointers.

1. Get a job in a department store for a company with little or no treatment products. A few companies I'm familiar with are MAC, Makeup Forever, and Smashbox. These are lines that encourage 'creativity.'

2. Go out on your own. Become a freelance makeup artist. To do this you will either need to hand out business cards to different counters and hope they call you if they have an event that requires a freelancer, or you can put together a kit complete with makeup brushes, eyeshadows, blushes, etc., and do what I do now—weddings and special occasion makeovers.

"The latter of the two is less expensive to start, but if you begin your career by working in a department store as a 'beauty adviser,' you will reap the benefits of gratis—free stuff! Most companies give a certain dollar amount (usually more for full-time workers) of gratis to each adviser. It's easy to make a kit this way so you can do special occasion makeovers as a side job."

How Mary Kern Got Started

"I have had an interest in cosmetics since I was fourteen years old, when my mother took me to the grocery store to buy me my first eye shadow and lipstick (that's as much as she would allow me to wear at the time). The eye shadow was a Maybelline shade in a lovely green frost, and the lipstick was a frosty pink—both of which I would not be caught dead wearing today!

"I received a B.A. (with honors) from Glassboro State College (which has since been renamed Rowan University) in 1991. My major was radio, television, and film. In the months before I graduated, I did an internship for a local cable station in the programming department part-time and at the same time worked part-time across the street at the Monmouth Mall (in Eatontown, New Jersey) in the men's department for a department store chain.

"When I completed the internship, I began my pursuit of a job in the television industry—to no avail. After almost a year of searching, I gave up and took on a full-time position at the department store. It was March of 1992. I had been engaged for three months, and I just figured I would put off the television career for a while—this way I could plan my wedding. After showing interest in the cosmetics department to the upper management of the department store I was working in, I landed a job as a 'beauty adviser' for Estee Lauder.

"In June of 1993, I went to work for Nordstrom as a business manager for a French line called Clarins. It wasn't terribly popular for its makeup at the time, so I grew bored very quickly.

"Nine months later I took a job as a beauty adviser for Lancôme. While it was a 'step down' in title, I earned a lot more money because of the popularity of the line. I also got a lot of gratis that I used to make a kit for myself, and, in April 1995, I did my first wedding makeover. I left Nordstrom in August of 1995 on maternity leave and returned again in January 1996."

Landing That Job—Interviewing Tips

"I was hired for all my jobs for a few reasons:

1. I showed overwhelming enthusiasm during my interview. You have to be upbeat and confident in all the answers you give the interviewer.

2. I am not squeamish when it comes to touching people's faces. It sounds odd, but I was asked that by the interviewer.

There are times when you have to deal with less than perfect skin and you can't refuse to do the makeup.

3. I 'looked the part.' If you want to work in cosmetics, you have to wear them and know what you're doing. The only way interviewers can tell if you know how to apply makeup well is by looking at what's in front of them. Subscribing to magazines such as *Mademoiselle*, *Allure*, and *Glamour*, getting tips, and practicing different looks on yourself as well as others (using family and friends as guinea pigs when possible) is a great way to get started. I had practiced this method since high school. I was so into it that one guy I graduated from high school with inscribed in my notebook 'Good luck in beauty school'—he must have been psychic!"

Breaking into Freelancing

"I found it difficult to balance a job and my new role as a mother, so I made the decision to leave Nordstrom in May 1996 and eventually pursued freelance opportunities.

"I started with Lancôme, in June of 1996, doing special events (i.e., 'Gift with Purchase') and have since worked for Makeup Forever and Borghese. My time has been limited for weddings and special occasions because of the work I've committed to do for these companies, as well as my responsibilities as a mother—which I take very seriously.

"This is a positive aspect of this industry for me (or other stay-at-home parents) because it is a good source of extra income and I am able to make my own hours. If I get a call for a wedding or event in a store, and I am unable to do it, I decline. However, there are freelancers who are able to book jobs for themselves every week within the department stores or who are booked almost every weekend with a wedding or other occasion."

The Approaches You Can Take

"For the person who might be looking toward being a makeup artist who specializes in weddings (or other occasions), it may take some more work, but the possibilities are endless.

1. You could go to a vocational beauty school and become a certified professional makeup artist.

2. You could obtain a business license and manage your own specialty beauty salon.

3. You could do it as a home-based business (maybe hiring out other freelancers to work for you).

4. You could work locally or within a certain area.

"Whatever choice you make, the demand is certainly out there. Although most weddings are on Friday night, Saturday, or Sunday, the weekdays of a person in this business can be spent doing makeovers for engagement parties or other special occasions or even 'preliminary looks.' Most brides like to have their makeup done by the makeup artist ahead of time to get an idea of how it might look for the wedding day. The makeup artists also benefit from doing this because they can get an idea of what the bride's likes and dislikes are."

The Finances Involved

"As far as the financial aspect of this work is concerned, pricing is entirely up to the individual makeup artist. Some artists who do special occasion makeovers charge anywhere from $40 to $125 per person (the majority charge $50).

"Some choose to charge more for the bride (because her makeup usually takes more time), and some will do the bride's makeup for free if the bride can guarantee a certain amount of people to do in the wedding party. Others charge more, depending on the commute."

Time Management

"Some artists will also limit the amount of people they will do. I can do as many as six makeovers per party, but I won't do less than two. Being organized is the key to a makeup artist's success. I allow at least half an hour per person from start to finish, and I always tack on an extra fifteen minutes to half an hour for traveling depending on my familiarity with the location, plus I give an extra half hour just in case someone is running late. Being organized and having the bride satisfied with the makeup artist's work means more work will follow because nine out of ten jobs are a result of referrals."

The Romance of the Job

"My favorite part of doing a wedding makeover is the romantic aspect of the job. There is always a hint of nervousness in the air that tends to take me back to my own wedding day. When the bride sits in my chair, she's usually got her hair done and her hairpiece and veil in place (hair always gets done first), so she's generally a little calmer because that part's finished. Now all she has left, before the photographer shows up, is for me to do her makeup and to get into her gown. I find that an organized bride is a calm bride. The few problems I've faced have been with brides who did not organize their time properly or who procrastinated before sitting down for makeup only to rush the most important step—mine! Unfortunately, I don't work well under pressure. To avoid rushing through the bride's makeover, I usually establish with her, ahead of time, that her makeup should be done first because of her importance that day and because once I'm finished with her, I can figure out the remaining time I will have to do the rest of the wedding party. Unfortunately, it doesn't always work out this way, but once the bride's makeup is finished, tensions usually ease a bit for everyone.

"I like to establish a friendly rapport with the bride to be before and during her special day. Sometimes they tell me about their husbands to be or confide in me about their hopes for the future. They ask me questions about my wedding. Usually I get to preview the gown. We talk about honeymoon destinations, and they tell me how nervous and excited they are. It makes me feel like an important part of their day. But my favorite part is when I am finished and everyone looks beautiful. The brides usually tell me how pleased they are (thankfully no one has ever told me she wasn't). Afterwards, I go home and generally spend my day thinking about the bride. I hope her makeup stays on well. I wonder how her day is going and how many people must be looking at her face and maybe are even commenting on her makeup. I'd like to think that years from now, when they look at their wedding pictures, they might remember me as a 'fairy godmother' of sorts who helped make part of their Cinderella dreams come true."

Kathleen Lucerne, Cosmetologist

Kathleen Lucerne is a cosmetologist, working in Sunrise, Florida. She has been in the business more than thirty years, both as a salon owner and operator and now as a freelancer.

Her training involved twelve hundred hours of cosmetology school, advanced hairstyling courses, and continuing education in the field.

The Lure of the Beauty Business

"What attracted me to the beauty business was that I always admired women who took care of themselves. As a child I used to love to set and fix all my family's hair, sitting for what seemed like hours, twisting each section of hair perfectly around my finger and making rows of pin curls.

"My first job was in a small salon that was owned and operated by a husband-and-wife team. The husband was quite arrogant! As he would be styling hair, he would constantly say 'now, watch me, watch how I do this,' and I would, and, being so very young, I thought 'I can do that!' As it turned out, it was my God-given talent, and he never asked me to watch him much after that.

"I then went on to own my own salon. But now, after thirty years, I am semiretired, and do what I like best! I love doing brides and the mothers of the bride, and the bridesmaids. I really love doing makeup and hair for special occasions. It makes me feel like a fairy godmother waving her wand!

"I think doing this kind of beauty work is much more exciting than the humdrum of the salon, day in and day out.

"I get most of my clients from referrals, word of mouth, but you can also advertise locally.

"I try to stay pretty local, but I will travel some if I have been requested by someone I have done business with before."

What the Job Involves

"What I do first is speak with the bride by phone and find out when the wedding is and how many people will want my services. I tell her to bring pictures and her veil when we meet, plus her personal makeup, if she has any at all.

"I will advise her if she is planning on getting a facial before her wedding to do that at least two weeks prior to the date.

"I can also give her advice on her hands—I do manicures also and put on what I call temporary nail tips that can be popped off in a matter of days. Many brides like to have their hands and their new hubby's hands photographed with their wedding bands on.

"Now, as for the makeup, it should be soft for the wedding day. But usually, the bridal portrait is done before the wedding and, in that case, the makeup for the eyes and lips can be a little bit more dramatic. I can and will use the individual's own personal makeup, and most of the time the bride will say to me, 'Why can't I do this?'

"I also do the bride's hair—and that is usually done the day before the wedding.

"Any fully licensed cosmetologist can do this, as a business or out of a beauty salon, but the latter would not allow you time for clients you would see in their homes. I have done whole wedding parties in my salon, but now I go to the home. Everyone must have their hair washed and dried when I arrive, and I go from there.

"The one thing you must remember to always have with you, though, is a pleasing, confident personality.

"For me it is a lot of fun. You feel the excitement and feel so fulfilled to make someone 'Queen for a Day.'"

The Finances Involved

"Prices can vary. You can charge a flat fee for your whole service or charge a separate price for each service you perform. Sometimes you might do their makeup and hair, or they might do their own and then you touch it up.

"How far I have to travel, what special or extra things will be needed, what supplies I will be using—this all gets calculated in. The fees could run from $35 a person to $75 or more, depending on what they will be getting done."

CHAPTER NINE

Say It with Pictures

One of the most romantic days in a couple's life is their wedding day. Wedding photographers and videographers help capture that special feeling. They take beautiful photographs or record the live events that, when viewed later, will bring back a flood of memories.

With some creativity, skill, and a passion to succeed, you can experience the romance of a wedding on a weekly basis—while earning a good living at the same time.

The Technicalities of the Work

Photographers use a wide variety of cameras that can accept lenses designed for close-up, medium-range, or distance photography. Some cameras also offer adjustment settings that allow the photographer greater creative and technical control over the picture-taking process. In addition to cameras and film, photographers and videographers use an array of equipment, from filters, tripods, and flash attachments to specially constructed lighting equipment.

Photography these days increasingly involves the use of computers. A photographer may take a picture, scan it to digital form, and, using a computer, manipulate it to create a desired effect. The images may be stored on a compact disc (CD) in the same way that music is stored on a CD.

Currently, some photographers use this technology to create an electronic portfolio. However, due to somewhat inferior image quality and high cost, this technology has not been widely adopted yet.

Videographers use video cameras to tape private ceremonies and special events, such as engagement parties and weddings. Making professional photographs and videos requires technical expertise and creativity. Composing a picture includes choosing and presenting a subject to achieve a particular effect and selecting equipment to accomplish the desired goal. By creatively using lighting, lenses, film, filters, and camera settings, photographers produce pictures that capture a mood or tell a story. For example, photographers may enhance the subject's appearance with lighting or by drawing attention to a particular aspect by blurring the background.

Some photographers develop and print their own photographs, especially those requiring special effects, but this requires a fully equipped darkroom and the technical skill to operate it. As a result, many professional photographers send their film to laboratories for processing. This is especially true for color film, which requires very expensive equipment and exacting conditions for processing and printing.

Specialties

Most photographers specialize in commercial, portrait, or media photography. Of the most interest to romantics is the specialty in wedding photography. Some photographers also specialize in school photographs.

Portrait Photographers

Portrait photographers take pictures of individuals or groups of people and often work in their own studios. Those who are business owners arrange for advertising, schedule appointments, set and adjust equipment, develop and retouch negatives, and mount and frame pictures. They also hire and train employees, purchase supplies, keep records, and bill customers.

Freelance Photographers

Freelance photographers may license the use of their photographs through stock photo agencies. These agencies grant magazines and other customers the right to purchase the use of a photograph and, in turn, pay the photographer on a commission basis. Stock photo agencies require an application from the photographer and a sizable portfolio. Once accepted, a large number of new submissions are generally required each year. Photographers frequently have their photos placed on CDs for this purpose.

Commercial and Industrial Photographers

Commercial and industrial photographers take pictures of such subjects as manufactured articles, buildings, livestock, landscapes, and groups of people. Their work is used in a wide variety of mediums, such as reports, advertisements, and catalogs. Industrial photographers use photographs or videotapes for analyzing engineering projects, publicity, or as records of equipment development or deployment, such as the placement of an offshore oil rig. Automobile manufacturers hire photographers every year to publicize their new models. Companies use photographs in publications to report to stockholders or to advertise company products or services. This photography is frequently done on location.

Scientific Photographers

Scientific photographers provide illustrations and documentation for scientific publications, research reports, and textbooks. They usually specialize in a field such as engineering, medicine, biology, or chemistry. Some use photographic or video equipment as research tools. For example, biomedical photographers use photomicrography, photographs of small objects magnified many times to obtain information not visible under normal conditions, and time-lapse photography, where time is stretched or condensed. Biomedical photographers record medical procedures such as surgery.

Photojournalists

Photojournalists photograph newsworthy events, places, people, and things for newspapers, journals, magazines, or television. Some are salaried staff, while others are independent and work as freelance photographers.

Fine Art Photographers

Photography also is an art medium. Some photographers sell their photographs as artwork, placing even greater emphasis on self-expression and creativity, in addition to technical proficiency. Unlike other specializations, however, very few artistic photographers are successful enough to support themselves in this manner.

Working Conditions

Working conditions for photographers vary considerably. Photographers employed in government, commercial studios, and advertising agencies usually work a five-day, forty-hour week.

Self-employment allows for greater autonomy, freedom of expression, and flexible scheduling. However, income is uncertain and necessitates a continuous, time-consuming, and sometimes stressful search for new clients. Some photographers hire an assistant solely for this responsibility. Portrait photographers often work in their own studios but may travel to take photographs at weddings and other events.

Some photographers have to stand or walk for long periods while carrying heavy equipment. Photographers often work under severe time restrictions to meet deadlines and satisfy customers.

Employment

Photographers hold about 140,000 jobs. About four out of ten photographers are self-employed, a much higher proportion than the average for all occupations.

Most salaried photographers work in portrait or commercial photography studios in metropolitan areas.

Training

Employers usually seek applicants with a good technical understanding of photography who are imaginative and creative. Although most wedding photographers are self-employed, many have apprenticed at commercial studios as photography assistants, often learning to mix chemicals, develop film, print photographs, and the various skills vital to running a business.

If you are interested in pursuing this occupation, you should subscribe to photographic newsletters and magazines, join camera clubs, and seek work in camera stores or photo studios.

You should also should decide on an area of interest and specialize in it. Completing a course of study at a private photographic institute, university, or community college provides many of the necessary skills to be successful. Summer or part-time work for a photographer, network, newspaper, or magazine is an excellent way to gain experience and eventual entry to this field.

Many sources, including universities, community and junior colleges, vocational-technical institutes, and private trade and technical schools offer courses in photography. Courses in cinematography are most often offered by photography institutes and universities. Many photographers enhance their technical expertise by attending seminars.

Basic courses in photography cover equipment, processes, and techniques. Bachelor's degree programs provide a well-rounded education, including business courses. Art schools offer useful training in design and composition but may be weak in the technical and commercial aspects of photography.

The Self-Employed Wedding Photographer

Photographers who wish to operate their own businesses need business skills as well as talent. They must know how to submit bids, write contracts, price their services, and keep financial records.

They should develop an individual style of photography to differentiate themselves from the competition. Most self-employed photographers develop a portfolio of previous work to show prospective clients.

The Personal Qualities You'll Need

Photographers also need good eyesight, artistic ability, and manual dexterity. They should be patient, accurate, and enjoy working with detail. They should be able to work alone or with others, as photographers frequently deal with clients, graphic designers, and advertising and publishing specialists. Knowledge of mathematics, physics, and chemistry is helpful for understanding the workings of lenses, films, light sources, and developing processes.

Most important, portrait photographers need the ability to help people relax in front of the camera.

Job Outlook

Photography is a highly competitive field because there are more people who want to be photographers than there is employment to support them. Only the most skilled and those with the best business ability and who have developed the best reputations in the industry are able to find salaried positions or attract enough work to support themselves as self-employed photographers.

Many have full-time jobs in other fields and take photographs or videos of weddings and other events on weekends.

Employment of photographers is expected to grow faster than the average for all occupations through the year 2005. The growing demand for visual images in education, communication, entertainment, marketing, research and development, and other areas should spur demand for photographers. Demand for portrait photographers should increase as the population grows.

Earnings

The median annual earnings for salaried photographers who worked full-time is only about $25,000.

Most salaried photographers work full-time and earn more than the majority of self-employed photographers who work part-time, but some self-employed photographers have very high earnings. Earnings are affected by the number of hours worked, skills, marketing ability, and general business conditions.

What It's Really Like

Ronald Rice, Wedding Photographer

Ronald Rice is a self-employed wedding photographer in Torrance, California. He has been in this line of work since

1977. Although he has a B.A. degree in psychology, all his photography skills are self-taught. You can learn more about him in the following interview and also at his website at http://members.aol.com/hastime4u/index.html.

The Attraction to the Field

"Being a people person and loving all living things, I decided that people pictures was my best avenue of pursuit.

"One evening I was showing some of my slides at a family reunion. My aunt was an art critic and writing a column in a local newspaper at the time. After seeing my slides, she immediately pointed out some interesting styles and composition in my pictures and the unique way that I had composed them. Ever since the day she told me I had potential for photographing, I became more realized and happy about the way I took photographs. I have my aunt to thank for encouraging me."

Getting Started

"My first job as a wedding photographer was a bittersweet experience. A friend of mine knew of someone who was planning a wedding and asked me if I'd be willing to shoot the ceremony and reception for $75. Naturally, being a photo bug and knowing I would get paid for it at the same time, I told him I would be delighted. I had my 35mm camera with a Sologar flash unit and thirteen rolls of film. I was shooting anyone and anything that moved! But when it came time for the bride and groom to start their wedding processional down the aisle, I suddenly noticed that my flash unit wasn't recycling fast enough to capture everyone. The butterflies were fluttering big time at this point. I knew that some of the pictures were not going to be properly exposed.

"However, maintaining my composure, with sweat dripping down my brow, I continued. I was well aware of the limitations of the photo equipment I was using. One week later and $10,000 poorer, with the money invested in camera and flash equipment, I was confident that the next wedding, if there was to be one, would be covered and exposed properly."

What the Job Involves

"It's like being invited to a party every weekend. Everyone is dressed up and happy. There is free food. And I get to do my most favorite thing—take pictures. I'm truly a blessed person.

"On the days I am not actually covering a wedding, I awake, take a shower, go to the gym, and eat breakfast. By 11 A.M., I'm in my car driving to the labs to expedite the printing of my wedding orders.

"If any orders are ready, I pick them up and return home and begin sorting and assembling wedding albums. I check my phone messages at various times during the day and return phone calls from people wanting information about wedding packages and plans. I will try to book an appointment for them to come see the wedding pictures I have on my walls and in my preview albums.

"Because I work at home, when there is a couple scheduled to come in and talk with me about their wedding plans and what they expect from their wedding photographer, I begin cleaning up my house, vacuuming, polishing, and dusting. I even burn incense to make my home as personable and relaxing for the visiting clients as I possibly can.

"Some days it will be so busy, and you will have no time for relaxing. However, there will be days when you have everything flowing smoothly, and this is the time when you can kick back and relax. I do much of my assembly of wedding albums during the late evening hours, so I can afford more leisure time during the daylight hours.

"The work is definitely interesting. However, it's dependent on what kind of person you are. For me it is the best and most rewarding job I have ever had, and I wouldn't trade it in for anything else.

"The only boring aspect of the wedding photographer's day is when the reception is moving extra slowly. But if you, like me, develop your wedding plans on an hour to hour schedule, you'll keep the boredom to a minimum.

"And, if you are creative, you can become a professional PR person during the down times. I will dance with the wedding guests—everyone loves to see the professional having fun, too—or I will search out couples at the reception and take their pictures. This will lead to more sales and greater profits. This way the boring times can be transformed into profit times.

"With my current work schedule, I will maybe put in a good twenty hours or more of work per week. When you are just starting out, though, you should expect to work forty plus hours, developing a client base and image profile for yourself.

"If you plan on having a retail store and personnel working for you and with you, then add at least ten to fifteen hours to your work week, if not more. It's a whole different ball game between retail locations and home-based locations."

The Romance of the Job

"The most rewarding part of being a wedding photographer is the satisfaction of seeing your clients laughing, crying, and making sounds of 'Oh, wow! Look at this one,' and it is the first and foremost reason for my getting into this profession. I love the feeling I get when people tell you how creative and distinctively romantic your wedding photographs are."

The Downsides

"The most difficult aspect of this work is when a couple over orders, thinking they can afford all the pictures but ending up not having the finances to cover the balance. And then you get stuck with the bill.

"Be very sure your clients know how much it will cost to obtain all the photographs they want. It's a rare occasion that the money issue comes up. But when it does, be ready to stand your ground. I have noticed in my years of shooting weddings that many people will try anything to get price breaks and extra generosity deals."

The Finances Involved

"You have to set your price range according to the location in which you are doing business. Different areas merit different prices. If I were just starting out, I'd start cheap and work my way up as more and more business came through the door. As I stated earlier, I charged $75 for my first wedding. I now charge anywhere from $595 to $2,200. But you need to have patience and work your way into the range that you think you're worth.

"I personally like a flexible pricing style, where all potential clients can have the opportunity to contract your services.

"You can earn a decent living doing this. And you can be happy providing photographs as romantic and as lovely as the wedding day itself. I average $1,500 dollars per wedding, sometimes more than that, if the coverage is a large one and there are many people attending."

Advice from Ronald Rice

"If you plan to maintain a profitable and successful wedding photography business, you'll need to invest at least 20 percent of your income into advertising. I can't stress enough the importance of investing in your advertising and image profiles.

"Be a good accountant and keep your records and books in perfect order. You can from time to time do some market research and analyze your best methods for making money and then accent them. You can also analyze what methods of your operation aren't doing well and either choose to delete them or refine them.

"When meeting with a potential client, you will need to be ready to give the best presentation possible. This includes having current samples of weddings you've done. To do that you can enlarge your best work and frame the prints and hang them up so you can have a gallery for the client to view.

"Without the passion for photography and communicative prowess and related skills, you would need to find another profession. Success requires a genuine love of yourself and others.

"As far as your art goes, be an individual! Be relaxed and have fun. This is the key to success in any venture you attempt.

"The job can be the best day of your life or the worst day. It's entirely up to you to create the outcome. The job is nerve-wracking and fun, problematic and challenging. It's all you want it to be."

CHAPTER TEN

Work with Honeymooners

O ut of all the industries worldwide, travel and tourism continue to grow at an astounding rate. Nearly everyone tries to take at least one vacation every year and many people travel frequently on business. Some travel for education, too, but it's that dreamy getaway, special honeymoon, or anniversary trip that would be of interest to you, someone wanting to combine your romantic instincts with a way to make a living.

At one time or another, most travelers seek out the services of a travel agent to help with all the details of a trip. This means that jobs for travel agents will continue to grow. Travel agents learn about all the different destinations, modes of transportation, hotels, resorts, and cruises, then work to match their customers' needs with the services travel providers offer.

Travel Agents

Travel agents generally work in an office and deal with customers in person or over the phone. They plot itineraries, make airline and hotel reservations, book passage on cruise ships, or arrange for car rentals.

But first of all, they listen to the needs of their customers then try to develop the best package for each person. They work with affluent, sophisticated travelers or first timers such as students trying to save money and travel on a budget. They could book a simple, round-trip air ticket for a person traveling alone or handle arrangements for hundreds of people traveling to attend a convention or conference.

Some travel agents are generalists; they handle any or all situations. Others specialize in a particular area such as cruise ships or corporate travel.

How a Travel Agent Gets the Job Done

Travel agents gather information from different sources. They use computer databases, attend trade shows, and read trade magazines. They also visit resorts or locations to get firsthand knowledge about a destination.

They have to keep up with rapidly changing fares and rates, and they have to know who offers the best packages and service. Their most important concern is the satisfaction of their customer. Happy customers come back again and refer friends and family.

The Upsides and Downsides

Most travel agents are offered "fam" trips to help familiarize them with a particular cruise line, safari adventure, exclusive resort, or ecological tour. These trips are offered free to the travel agent so they can "test-drive" a destination before suggesting it to their customers. Travel providers understand that a travel agent is more likely to sell what he or she knows and has enjoyed.

Travel agents also receive discounted travel on other business trips, as well as on their own vacations.

The downside, however, according to many travel agents, is that they seldom have enough free time to do all the traveling they would like. They are often tied to their desks, especially during peak travel periods, such as the summer or important busy holidays.

And the work can be frustrating at times. Customers might not always know what they want, or their plans can change, and, as a result, the travel agent might have to cancel or reroute destinations that had already been set.

Earnings for Travel Agents

Salary varies according to the region in which you work and your experience. Depending on the agency, you could start out on an hourly wage or a yearly salary. Some travel agents prefer to work on a commission basis. That way, the more trips they sell, the more money they earn. A salary plus commission is the best combination to work toward.

Travel agents who are good salespeople can also earn bonuses or more free or discounted trips. If your pay is initially low, it can be offset by this added benefit.

Getting Started

A four-year college degree is not necessary to become a travel agent. It can be helpful, however, and shows commitment and discipline. Most travel agents study for at least two years and earn an associate's degree. Many community colleges, trade and vocational schools offer good programs in travel and tourism or hospitality management.

Some travel agencies are willing to hire inexperienced applicants and provide them with their own training.

For a list of schools offering certified programs, you can write to the American Society of Travel Agents or the Institute of Certified Travel Agents. (The addresses are listed in Appendix A.)

What You Can Do to Get a Head Start

In school you need to stay awake during geography, history, and social studies classes and to keep a good eye on the newspaper and the nightly news. It's important to have an understanding of what's happening in the world around you. This will not only help you eventually learn how to sell a vacation, but it will help you to sell the *right* vacation. Informed travel agents, for example, make sure they don't send vacationers to an area of the world where there's a conflict going on.

Through public-speaking classes in school, you can gain self-confidence and become comfortable working with other people. It's also a good idea to get some retail sales experience. You could get a part-time job at the mall or do some telephone or customer relations work.

Travel agents are required to learn a computerized reservation system. You can start by becoming familiar with computers and databases. Most important, you can start sharpening your listening skills.

Below is a list of the qualities a good travel agent should demonstrate.

- *Have good communications skills.* You have to be able to listen well and understand the concerns and special needs of your customers.

- *Have an understanding of finances.* You'll need to work on your math skills to handle billing and collecting funds for the various fares and reservations.

- *Be a people person.* The customer comes first. You need to be someone who is genuinely friendly and enjoys working with all types of people.

- *Be a problem solver.* Arranging vacations and business trips can be like solving a big jigsaw puzzle. You have to be good at fitting all the pieces together.

- *Be detail oriented.* There's a lot of detail work in the travel business. You have to be conscientious and remember to dot all your *i*s and cross your *t*s.

- *Be well organized.* You have to be able to recognize priorities and manage your time well.

- *Be a good researcher and studier.* You have to read a lot and study the industry so you can match the client's desires with the best deals being offered.

- *Have patience.* No matter how good your intentions, things don't always run as smoothly as you would like. It's important not to get rattled easily.

What It's Really Like

Vivian Portela Buscher, Travel Agent

Vivian Portela Buscher started out as a ticket agent and in passenger services for the airlines, then she moved to a well-known cruise line as a booking agent. It was a natural progression for her to become a travel agent specializing in cruise travel and she has worked for the same agency now since 1987.

"Basically, what I do is this: people call me who have an interest in taking a cruise vacation, and I find for them the right cruise at the right price," Vivian says. "I think of it more as a matching game rather than a selling situation. My office doesn't call anyone asking them to buy a cruise; everyone calls us.

"I specifically chose to be a travel agent because working with the airlines had been becoming more and more difficult. You had to wait a long time to gain seniority and to have a comfortable work schedule with Saturdays and Sundays off. Plus, with so many airlines going out of business, there are a lot of unemployed people in the industry. The airline I worked for folded ten years ago, and I was happy to switch to the cruise business. I was looking for a job that would still be in the travel industry but that would be more secure and with normal hours.

"I work Monday through Friday, and since our agency is open from 9:00 A.M. to 9:00 P.M., I get to choose my hours during the day. Most people prefer to work earlier hours, but I don't. Basically, I work from 10:30 A.M. to 7:00 P.M."

How Vivian Got Started

"When I went to college I studied air carrier management and received a bachelor's degree in transportation management. My experience with the airlines and then with the cruise line also was important in preparing me. The rest I picked up through on-the-job training.

"Getting my first job was interesting. A friend of mine was offered the job first, but it wasn't the right location for her. She knew I had the same background and experience, so she referred me to the agency.

"The operations manager interviewed me over the telephone. He asked me about my background and then told me he was very interested and asked if I could start right away. We set up an in-person interview for the next day, but, because he already knew about my experience, during the interview he told me about the agency and what my duties and salary would be. I began work one week later.

"My first day was hectic. It was an office with a very high call volume and not a lot of employees at that time. The company has grown tremendously since I've been there, but at the time they were understaffed, and the phones were ringing, and they were just in the process of reorganizing the office. I walked in cold, and they told me to start answering the phones. I had no idea what I was supposed to say. At first I took the calls and passed messages onto the other agents. Then I started taking down more information, asking the customers what they needed, and started getting that information for them myself.

"There was a lot of new information I had to learn, a lot of intensive studying I had to do to acquire all the product knowledge about all the different cruise lines and packages. It was busy but exciting."

The Upsides

"I like to travel. I enjoy being involved with jobs related to travel. It's easy for me to advise other people about travel because it's something I like to do. There's a lot of satisfaction when some-one calls me back and tells me that the cruise was exactly as I had described it and that it was the best vacation of his or her life.

"You also get to travel yourself, to sample all the cruises and be more informed on them. I've been to Saint Thomas, San Juan, Nassau, Grand Cayman, Jamaica, Saint Lucia, to name just a few. We also get to attend a lot of luncheons and dinners and other inaugural activities to view the new ships when they come in.

"I can't think of one negative aspect to my work. I love it."

Advice from Vivian Portela Buscher

I think it's important to go to college and to get as much train-ing as you can and then to apply to work for an agency where you can get experience. Even if you get experience without going to school, it's very competitive. Sometimes the person with the most education will get the job over someone with equal experience.

"Most travel agents are paid on a combination of salary plus commission. Sometimes you also get bonuses—maybe $25 to $100 for every cabin you book. It depends what the particular cruise line is promoting. I'm paid completely on commission, which is something I chose to do. The more you sell the more you earn."

Mary Fallon Miller, Travel Agent

Mary Fallon Miller started her career as a travel agent in 1986 when she opened her own agency. In partnership with her broth-er, a captain in the merchant marines, Mary first focused on bus tours, transporting groups to see special events in her area. She later moved on to specialize in cruise travel.

"At the age of seven I sailed across the Atlantic on the S.S. France, and then, later, as a young woman, I accompanied my mother throughout Europe and South America," Mary recalls. "I fell in love with the glamour and excitement of travel. It gets in your blood; I have a real fascination for other cultures and languages. I realized that a career as a travel agent would allow me to pursue my dream to see more of the world.

"But when you're just starting out, you're tied to the office and the computer a lot. A newcomer would get to take at least one week a year, more once you've gained some seniority. The owners of a travel agency get to go on more 'fam' trips, but if someone just starting out is seen as a productive member of the business, helping to build it, he or she would get more opportunities. You'll be the one they send on the 'cruise-a-thon' or to the ski shows, and then you'll become your agency's representative."

The Upsides

"Having a passenger or a guest that's happy is what gives me the most satisfaction. Having a honeymoon trip that's successfully done, having a group of people come back over and over and recommend you to their friends. What could be more flattering?"

The Downsides

"The most difficult part of the work is keeping all the details accurate and being able to deal with what we call 'grumps and whiners.' There are people who get very nervous about their travel arrangements, and they can complain and make your life miserable. But you have to be able to be compassionate—find out *why* they're so concerned. Maybe they had a bad experience in the past. You have to try to know as much about your client as possible.

"And there are times when things go wrong. There could be a snow-in at an airport and people miss their connections, or someone in the family dies and they have to cancel the whole cruise reservation at the last minute. You have to be professional and flexible, and you have to be on the ball all the time.

"It's a demanding job, but it's satisfying. People come back and say, 'I can't believe you knew exactly what I wanted. That's the best vacation I've ever had. And I'm telling all my friends.' You start getting more and more customers coming in, and they ask for you by name. That feels really good. You're making a dream come true, and, in a way, that's what you're doing—selling dreams."

Getting Started

"Beginners would probably start working side by side with someone more experienced in the agency. They might be placed in a specific department handling, for example, European travel or cruises or car rentals and airfares. Much of their time will be spent coordinating and arranging details."

A Typical Day

"Here's how an average day as a travel agent might progress.

- 9:00 A.M.—I return a phone call to Mr. and Mrs. Jones to tell them I was able to get them a great cabin. We discuss which seating time for dinner they prefer, and I ask them if they're celebrating any birthdays. (If they are, the cruise staff will provide a birthday cake.) I let them know when they'll get their tickets and on what date their deposit is due.

- 9:30 A.M.—A call comes in from a John and Sue who are getting married. They want to know about a hotel that provides a reception hall, and then they want me to book their flight to Aruba for their honeymoon.

- 10:00 A.M.—I make a few phone calls to different hotels and the airlines, and then I call the couple back with confirmations.

- 11:00 A.M.—Another couple telephones to ask if I can find them a resort that caters to young people. They want to go to the Virgin Islands and ask about passport requirements and if they need any inoculations.

- noon—I make a few phone calls on their behalf to see what's available.

- 1:30 P.M.—After lunch I do some research at my desk reading brochures and trade magazines such as *Travel Weekly* and *Travel Agent*.

- 2:30 P.M.—I confirm a few details on a cruise I booked the day before, then I begin work developing a roster list. One hundred people are traveling by bus to Miami, and then they'll hook up with their cruise. I have to make sure all their names are correct and that their hotel rooms are all booked.

- 4:00 P.M.—IBM called to book a hotel for a convention. I have to take down all the details, how many rooms they'll need and for how many nights. We also discuss the budget and what we expect the cost to run. I spend the rest of the day contacting various hotels. I'll call IBM back in the morning to give them a few choices.

Advice from Mary Fallon Miller

"Read *Time, Newsweek,* and your local newspaper. Try to stay in touch with the world. Listen to National Public Radio or watch the Travel Channel on television.

"Don't be afraid of learning the computer, study languages, and, if you have the chance, participate in college language clubs or take advantage of a foreign exchange program. I lived in Poland for a summer.

"Most important, learn communication skills. And, at the beginning, when you're doing some of the drudgery work, it helps to remember that down the road you will receive discounts and free travel, that you have something you are working toward. The hard work will pay off."

Romantic Retreats

Many entrepreneurial romantics have been caught up in a popular movement throughout the country—restoring and refurbishing historic homes and converting them into country inns, guest houses, and bed-and-breakfast establishments.

Although nothing could be more romantic than a charming hideaway for a honeymooning couple or vacationing lovers, the reality is that running such an establishment is plain, hard work. Learn what it is like firsthand from innkeepers Roger and Mary Schmidt.

What It's Really Like

Roger and Mary Schmidt, Innkeepers

Roger and Mary Schmidt own an inn, called simply the 18 Gardner Street Inn, on Nantucket, an island about thirty miles off the coast of Massachusetts. "A lot of people want to live out their romantic dream," explains Roger Schmidt, "by retiring to an idyllic spot such as Nantucket and running a bed-and-breakfast. But the first major mistake they make is when they use the word 'retiring.' There's nothing retiring, or romantic, about operating an inn. You have to work very hard."

The Schmidt's colonial-style house, which is on the island's historical walking tour, was originally built in 1835 by Captain Robert Joy. The sea captain took the proceeds of his last whaling excursion and built the house for his retirement. Over the years the home was owned by several different families. In the 1940s, the property was converted to a lodging house with six or seven rooms. The next family that purchased the inn installed bathrooms in the rooms and ran it as a bed-and-breakfast.

Nantucket is a wonderful place to be an inn owner. Tourism supports the seven thousand or so year-round residents (the summer population blossoms to near forty thousand each year). Many of the historic homes on the island, Quaker-style, simple but sturdy dwellings, and the perfectly preserved Georgian, Federal, and Greek Revival-style houses have been converted into guest houses or bed-and-breakfasts.

Some of the houses are impressive mansions, the legacy of the wealth-producing whaling industry. Others are small, dollhouse-like affairs with geranium-filled planter boxes sitting below lacy-curtained leaded glass windows. A glimpse inside any of the homes reveals old-world mahogany antiques—carved sea chests and canopied or sleigh beds, many with shiny brass or even solid silver fixtures. White wicker rockers grace wooden porches and widow's walks curve around under cedar-shake roof shingles.

The Nantucket Historical Association has a strong influence, and strict building codes are enthusiastically adhered to by residents. Though other tourist spots are often marred by lines of fast-food stands and high-rise hotels, no intrusive golden arches or glaring neon signs are allowed on the island. Even the gas stations are disguised, their red brick structures blending perfectly with their surroundings.

Restoring the Inn at 18 Gardner Street

The Schmidts acquired their inn in 1988. The building is a traditional square box shape with a pitched roof and an ell in the back where the kitchen was added in the late 1800s. In front, there's a center door with original hand-rolled glass windows on each side. A typical Nantucket friendship staircase graces the front door, with steps on either side meeting at the landing at the top. Weathered cedar shakes (which, along with the famous Nantucket fog, help to contribute to the island's other nickname, the "Grey Lady") and a large widow's walk complete the picture of an elegant sea captain's mansion.

Spread through the inn's two stories and finished third floor attic are twelve guest rooms furnished with pencil post, canopied, and four-poster beds and antique mahogany or cherry dressers and nightstands. All of the rooms are airy, and many are spacious suites, most with working fireplaces.

Roger and Mary and their two children occupy a two-bedroom apartment in the finished basement. During the first two years they owned the inn, the Schmidts completely refurnished it. In the third and fourth years, they started doing massive restoration to the guest rooms. They took all the wallpaper down and repaired the dozens of cracks they discovered in the plaster. They upgraded the bathrooms and, keeping the period appearance to the bedrooms, rewallpapered with pastels and satin wall coverings.

"We completely gutted the kitchen," Roger says, "and replaced it with a new commercial kitchen so we could serve guests a full breakfast. And, as so often happens in old houses, we discovered a beautiful fireplace hidden for years behind one of the plaster walls. Every three years or so, the exterior of the house gets a new paint job."

One thing the Schmidts avoided was putting up new walls. "We specifically chose an inn that wouldn't require massive reconstruction work. From experience, we learned that putting up sheet rock can get unbelievably expensive and complicated, dealing with commercial building codes. Because our property had been licensed for so many years as an inn, we didn't have to be relicensed, although we do have to get an annual license through the local building inspector."

How the Schmidts Got Started

The Schmidts are originally from Springfield, in western Massachusetts. "We honeymooned on Nantucket in 1977," Roger says, "and fell in love with the island. We then started coming three and four times a year. But when we started hunting for property to buy, it soon became obvious that the selling prices were way out of our reach.

"In the early eighties, property on Nantucket skyrocketed. I was in the electronics field, Mary worked in a photography lab, and the dream of owning a summer home got pushed aside because of economics. We went to the nearby island of Martha's Vineyard because we'd heard there were good buys there. We ended up finding some property there and got into the real estate business. We bought a mariner's home and completely restored it and turned it into a small, five-bedroom inn and developed some other pieces of property there, as well. This was all happening while we were still considering Springfield as our main residence.

"Eventually, we sold it all off and came back to Nantucket in a much better financial condition to buy our current property."

Avoiding the Pitfalls

"We had an innkeeper running 18 Gardner Street for us for two years, but we almost went bankrupt because of mismanagement," Roger says. "So, in April of 1990, we moved to the island permanently and took over running the inn. Business then took off like a cannonball. As terrible as this may sound, anybody who gets into this business and thinks success means serving the greatest cup of coffee and greeting every guest with a warm smile is totally wrong. It's not enough. You have to sell your property to a person on the other end of the phone. Unfortunately, for that person, he doesn't know what he's getting. He can't see it and touch it. So through written advertisements, in major newspapers such as the *Boston Globe* and the *New York Times*, and through verbal communications you have to get across to your potential guests what your facilities are. Then, when they come, you can give them the greatest cup of coffee and the warmest smile.

"But that's still not enough. You have to understand your guests' needs and try to meet them. For example, we listened to our guests and learned that it was an inconvenience for them to have to walk downtown to pick up their rented bicycles. So we bought bicycles and provide them to our guests free of charge. We also learned that in the autumn it could be a long cold walk back from town, so that's when we made sure all our fireplaces were working. That keeps the fall business coming in. Again, we listened and learned that guests would like a little more than a muffin and coffee for breakfast. So, we got a food service permit and offer a full meal in the morning. We also provide dockside shuttle service from the ferry to the inn, picnic baskets, beach blankets, and ice coolers. We do what we can to make our guests happy. This has helped to substantially build up our word-of-mouth referral business.

"From April 1 to November 31, my day is primarily involved with taking reservations and handling problems and delegating responsibilities to our staff of five. During the winter, we involve ourselves with marketing and interior design and restoration. We're always busy."

Advice on Finances

"In 1988, we paid $850,000 for our historic inn, and at the time, that was a good price. The property dropped in value to $600,000 in the next two years, but now, because of the restoration and the steady clientele we've built up, our property and our business are worth slightly over $1 million.

"Right now our rooms are full about a hundred days of the year, and we are aiming to have full occupancy every weekend through the off-season months. The inn is an upscale one, and our high-season rates are from $140 to $170 a night. But our monthly operating expenses and our mortgage payments are very high, too.

"Nantucket, of course, is a small and very expensive island. There are many areas in the country where you could pick up a small house or an established inn for around $100,000.

"Whatever the value, the trick is to have an understanding of real estate financing and to try to be a little creative. In our case, we put very little down; the owner was willing to hold back a second mortgage. Another alternative is to lease with an option to buy. We've just done that with the property adjoining ours, and now we have five more guest rooms to book.

"But I would advise starting out with a property with just three or four guest rooms. It's a very risky business, and there's a high burnout and turnover rate. Sometimes the dream can turn into a nightmare. You can't treat it as a dream. You have to treat it as a business."

Romantic Rides

Perhaps where you live or when you've been on vacation, you've happened upon a colorful horse-drawn carriage holding a romantic couple taking a tour of the city. The atmosphere is festive, the driver looks regal in his livery, and everyone is having fun.

Although there's a lot of romance to such a trade, there's not a lot of mystery to get yourself started. Whether you live in St. Augustine, New Orleans, or New York City, as long as tourists regularly visit your locale, you can become your own horse-and-buggy tour operator.

What It's Really Like

Tom Doyle, Carriage Tour Owner

Tom Doyle owns such a business, the Palmetto Carriage Works, a horse- and mule-drawn carriage tour company in historic Charleston, South Carolina.

Tom's tours are an hour long and cover twenty blocks of the old city. Drivers provide a nonstop narration about Charleston's history, architecture, gardens, people, and points of interest.

"As opposed to a motorized tour, our drivers can turn and talk to the people and make eye contact," Tom Doyle explains. "It's a leisurely business. While you're waiting for the carriage to fill up, you chat with the passengers. To have a really great tour you need to get to know your customers. And tourists are great to deal with, because 99.9 percent of them are in a good mood. They're on vacation after all! When I take people on a carriage tour, everyone in the city benefits, because I leave them so happy with Charleston, they're wanting to do more and to come back."

Choosing Your Animals and Equipment

"There's nothing better than a good mule, and there's nothing worse than a bad one," says Tom. "The thing about the bad ones, though, is that they don't hide it very well. I can spend an afternoon with a mule and know whether or not it's going to work. A horse will go by something ninety-nine times as if it wasn't there, but on the hundredth time, the time you're not paying attention, the horse will absolutely freak out. Mules are much easier to train."

And if anyone should know the characteristics of mules, it's Tom Doyle. He has built up his tour business and now employs twenty-eight people, owns a stable right in the heart of the city, and has twenty-six carriages, two horses, and twenty-eight mules.

"The fellow who began the business started off with just the frame of an old farm wagon. He built some seats and a roof on top of it. He also had a carriage from the Jack Daniels Brewery, and he picked up a few old carriages from auctions. But they're not really built heavy duty enough for the kind of work we use them for, and they're too small. It's hard to find an antique carriage that will carry six or sixteen people. Because of that, we began designing our own carriages."

Tom employs one person who does nothing but build carriages. He also has a full barn staff, an office manager, a bookkeeper, a secretary, a ticket collector, and drivers who also double as grooms. But everyone is also a licensed tour guide. "The key to doing well in the carriage business," Tom explains, "is when the business is here, you've got to be able to handle it, and when it's not here, you have to be able to get real small. We're very seasonal."

Getting Started in the Carriage Trade

Tom Doyle came to Charleston from Massachusetts to study at the Citadel. When he finished with his B.A. in history, he looked around for work he would enjoy. But most of the things he liked to do didn't pay enough money to support a family, so he was often forced to hold down two jobs. Out of this moonlighting, he discovered the Palmetto Carriage Works and started as a part-time carriage driver-cum-tour guide. Within a year, however, he had graduated to full-time and was working sixty to seventy hours a week. When the original owner decided it was time to retire, in 1982, he offered the business to Tom. "I didn't have a dime at the time," Tom admits, "but he gave me such a good deal, I was able to go out and find some other people who were willing to invest, and I put together a little group of silent partners.

"It's possible to start small in this business," Tom maintains. "You don't need an office or a ticket collector or a fleet of carriages. With an investment of about $6,000, for the carriage, the tack, the animal and various permits, you can position yourself in a place that's visible to tourists—outside a visitor's information center or a popular place to stay or visit. "It's a see-and-do thing," says Tom. "The carriages themselves are the best advertising. Tourists will ask the driver, 'Hey, how do I get on one of these?'"

Marketing Yourself

"To make it work, you have to live the business," Tom warns. "You have to be out there driving every day, making friends, and getting to know everyone. Then word of mouth will get you going."

Tom also markets his business to the big hotels in town and the meeting planners and has found his niche with large groups. "People come into town for a conference or some other event, and they might want to do an off-premises function, maybe have dinner at a historic building. I tell them, 'Well, here's what we'll do. We'll pick you up in carriages and transport you there.' "

Tom also runs a free shuttle service with his 1934 antique Ford bus. He moves his customers from the visitor's center to his starting point. "But the real bread and butter of the business is the walk-up tourist."

A Few Golden Rules

To have a successful business, you must love the city where you're set up, and you have to be an expert and know everything about its local history. "Good business sense is also important," Tom says, "and, when you're the boss, you have to monitor your drivers—the tour they give is the most important part. I occasionally pay strangers to ride and check out the drivers."

Tom is convinced that it's more than a job—it's a lifestyle. "You get to work with the animals, which I really like. You can bring your children to work. All the neighborhood kids come around the stables to help out and get free rides. You have to do a good job. You're not only representing yourself, you're representing the whole city."

Where to Find That Carriage

"If you can find an Amish settlement, you'll be able to find carriages and farm wagons for sale," Tom says.

There are large Amish settlements in Pennsylvania, Indiana, Ohio, and Tennessee. To help locate these settlements, write or call the state's department of tourism, and the staff there will be able to direct you.

Professional Associations

C ontact the following organizations for more information about careers in each field.

For Writers

American Society of Journalists and Authors
1501 Broadway
New York, NY 10036
   A professional association for seasoned journalists and authors.

Fiction Writer's Connection
P.O. Box 4065
Deerfield Beach, FL 33442
   Provides free critiquing and advice to new writers.

Romance Writers of America
13700 Veterans Memorial Drive, Suite 316
Houston, TX 77014
   See Chapter 3 for a detailed description of RWA benefits.

For Floral Careers

American Association of Nurserymen
1250 Eye Street NW, Suite 500
Washington, DC 20005

Director of Educational Programs
American Floral Services, Inc.
P.O. Box 12309
Oklahoma City, OK 73157

American Floral Art School
529 South Wabash Avenue, #600
Chicago, IL 60605-1679

American Florists Association
2525 Heathcliff
Reston, VA 22091

American Institute of Floral Designers
720 Light Street
Baltimore, MD 21230-3816

Society of American Florists
1601 Duke Street
Alexandria, VA 22314-3406

For Wedding Consultants and Event Planners

Association of Bridal Consultants
200 Chestnutland Road
New Milford, CT 06776-2521
E-mail: BridalAssn@aol.com

The Association of Bridal Consultants is a membership service organization, designed to increase awareness of the wedding business and improve the professionalism of its members.

Membership benefits include advertising, referrals, insurance, and discounts on books and services.

Weddings Beautiful
3122 West Cary Street
Richmond, VA 23221-3504
E-mail: 104664.3577@compuserve.com
    Membership benefits include authorization to use "Member of Weddings Beautiful, America's Leading Wedding Coordinators" in your advertising; bridal leads; syndicated newspaper column to run under your name in local paper; bimonthly newsletter; consulting service; financial recommendations for consulting fees, rehearsals, etc.; various booklets on topics of interest to wedding professionals; training programs; and various other benefits.

    For information on certification and careers as an event planner contact:

The International Special Events Society
9202 North Meridean Street, Suite 200
Indianapolis, IN 46260

For Cosmetologists

A list of licensed training schools and licensing requirements for cosmetologists can be obtained from:

National Accrediting Commission of Cosmetology Arts and
    Sciences
901 North Stuart Street, Suite 900
Arlington, VA 22203

Association of Accredited Cosmetology Schools, Inc.
5201 Leesburg Pike
Falls Church, VA 22041

Information about cosmetology schools also is available from:

Accrediting Commission of Career Schools/Colleges of
    Technology
750 First Street NE, Suite 905
Washington, DC 20002

For details on state licensing requirements and approved barber or cosmetology schools, contact the state board of barber examiners or the state board of cosmetology in your state capital.

For Photographers

For reprints of a publication describing the work of various types of photographers and lists of colleges and universities offering courses or a degree in photography, write to:

American Society of Media Photographers
Washington Road, Suite 502
Princeton Junction, NJ 08550-1033

For more information on careers in photography, contact:

Professional Photographers of America, Inc.
57 Forsythe Street, Suite 1600
Atlanta, GA 30303

For Travel Agents

American Society of Travel Agents
1101 King Street
Alexandria, VA 22314

Association of Retail Travel Agents
1745 Jefferson Davis Highway, Suite 300
Arlington, VA 22202

Institute of Certified Travel Agents
148 Linden Street
P.O. Box 56
Wellesley, MA 02181

Cruise Line International Association
500 Fifth Avenue, Suite 1407
New York, NY 10110

Related Reading and Other Resources

T he following publications and resources will help you hone your romantic notions into marketable skills.

For Writers

These guides will show you where and how to submit your work.

- *Guide To Literary Agents & Art/Photo Representatives.* In addition to more than five hundred listings of fee-charging and nonfee-charging agents and what they handle, this annual guide also showcases several articles of interest to writers. Because the articles provide timeless information, it is a good idea to obtain a new edition each year and keep past editions for reference. One article of particular note in the 1994 edition, "How to Find (and Keep) the Right Agent," by agency head Lori Perkins, offers a comprehensive look at what agents do and how to get them to work for your best interests. (Writer's Digest Books)

- *Novel & Short Story Writer's Market.* This annual guide provides more than 1,900 entries of fiction publishing opportunities including the big houses, small presses, consumer magazines, and literary and small circulation magazines. The guide also offers advice and inspiration from top editors and authors. Here is a sampling. In the 1997 edition, you will find an article on "The Tools of the Trade" by authors Blythe Camenson and Marshall J. Cook, covering query letters, synopses, pitches, and cover letters. In the 1994 edition, Nora Roberts discusses making the switch from category to mainstream; Ann Hood explores the writer as his or her own best critiquer; Madge Harrah tells us "How to Handle Description"; and Sarah Orwig gives help on "Writing the Big Scene." Also included is a commercial fiction report devoted to what's happening in the publishing industry—including romance, mystery, and science fiction genres. (Writer's Digest Books)

For Flower Lovers

- *Careers for Plant Lovers*, by Blythe Camenson (NTC/Contemporary Publishing Group)

- *Opportunities in Horticulture Careers*, by Jan Goldberg (NTC/Contemporary Publishing Group)

- *PFD—Professional Floral Design*, *Floral Finance*, and *Retail Florist* are three monthlies available through AFS, P.O. Box 12309, Oklahoma City, OK 73157.

For Chocolate Lovers

- Subscribe to a newsletter about the world of chocolate. Contact Richard Pearlman Chocolates, 2550 Shattuck Avenue, #72, Berkeley, CA 94704.

For Wedding Planners

- *Special Events Magazine.* Available from Miramar Communications, 23815 Stuart Ranch Road, Malibu, CA 90265.

- *The Wedding Workshop.* The easiest and most up-to-date Windows-based wedding and special event–planning software on the market today. Records every detail from gifts to out-of-town guests; details expenses; handles multiple weddings; prints labels; addresses envelopes; provides more than 20,000 reports at the touch of a button. E-mail: sci1996@aol.com.

- http://www.wwsites.com/MA/illusions is the website for Illusions, the bridal shop featured in Chapter 6.

For Photographers

- http://members.aol.com/hastime4u/index.html is the website for wedding photographer Ronald Rice, profiled in Chapter 9.

For Travel Planners

- *How to Get a Job with a Cruise Line,* by Mary Fallon Miller. Includes descriptions of all the various jobs, an inside look at the different cruise lines, interviews with cruise personnel, and valuable tips on how to go about getting a job. Available from Ticket to Adventure Publishing, P.O. Box 41005, St. Petersburg, FL 33743-1005.

For Innkeepers

- *How to Start and Run a Bed & Breakfast Inn*, by Ripley Hotch and Carl Glassman. Covers buying the right inn, attracting guests, and estimating costs and profitability. (Stackpole Books)

- *The Seventh Old House Catalog*, by Lawrence Grow. An A to Z sourcebook for restoration and remodeling. (Sterling/Main Street Publishing)

About the Author

A full-time writer of career books, Blythe Camenson is mainly concerned with helping job seekers make educated choices. She firmly believes that with enough information, readers can find long-term, satisfying careers. To that end, she researches traditional as well as unusual occupations, talking to a variety of professionals about what their jobs are really like. In all of her books, she includes firsthand accounts from people who can reveal what to expect in each occupation,

Blythe Camenson was educated in Boston, earning her B.A. in English and psychology from the University of Massachusetts and her M.Ed. in counseling from Northeastern University.

In addition to *Careers for Romantics and Other Dreamy Types*, she has written more than thirty books for NTC/Contemporary Publishing Group.